Routledge Revivals

Mutual Aid Universities

First published in 1984, this collection of essays was the first account of the development of the University of the Third Age in Britain (U3A). Changing employment patterns and increasing pressure on traditional areas of secondary and higher education has led to the idea that learning can be a life-long process. The theories of U3As in Britain, their development under the influence of European models, and the major influences on them are analysed. The authors argue that the consequences of social change and the economic, social, political, sexual and racial inequalities that exist are often reinforced by the inequalities in our educational system. A comprehensive title, this book will be useful to students with an interest in adult and continuing education.

Mutual Aid Universities

Edited by
Eric Midwinter

Routledge
Taylor & Francis Group

First published in 1984
by Croom Helm Ltd

This edition first published in 2015 by Routledge
2 Park Square, Milton Park, Abingdon, Oxon, OX14 4RN
and by Routledge
711 Third Avenue, New York, NY 10017

Routledge is an imprint of the Taylor & Francis Group, an informa business

Publisher's Note
The publisher has gone to great lengths to ensure the quality of this reprint but
points out that some imperfections in the original copies may be apparent.

Disclaimer
The publisher has made every effort to trace copyright holders and welcomes
correspondence from those they have been unable to contact.

A Library of Congress record exists under LC control number: 84014988

ISBN 13: 978-1-138-82365-5 (hbk)
ISBN 13: 978-1-315-74195-6 (ebk)
ISBN 13: 978-1-138-82366-2 (pbk)

Mutual Aid Universities

Edited by
Eric Midwinter

CROOM HELM
London • Sydney • Dover, New Hampshire

© 1984 E. Midwinter
Croom Helm Ltd, Provident House, Burrell Row,
Beckenham, Kent BR3 1AT
Croom Helm Australia Pty Ltd, First Floor, 139 King St.,
Sydney, NSW 2001, Australia
Croom Helm, 51 Washington Street, Dover,
New Hampshire 03820, USA

British Library Cataloguing in Publication Data

Mutual aid universities.
    1. Education of the aged.—Great Britain
    I. Midwinter, Eric
    374   LC5219

    ISBN 0-7099-3523-4

Library of Congress Cataloging in Publication Data

Main entry under title:
Mutual aid universities.

    Includes index.
    1. Adult education – Great Britain – Addresses,
essays, lectures. 2. Education of the aged – Great
Britain – Addresses, essays, lectures. 3. Continuing
education – Great Britain – Addresses, essays, lectures.
4. Universities and colleges – Great Britain – Addresses,
essays, lectures. 5. Peer-group tutoring of students –
Addreses, essays, lectures. I. Midwinter, Eric C.
LC5256.G7M87 1984   374'.941   84-14988
ISBN 0-7099-3523-4

Printed and bound in Great Britain by
Biddles Ltd, Guildford and King's Lynn

CONTENTS

PART 1.　THE GENERAL: BACKGROUND AND DEVELOPMENT

Chapter 1

UNIVERSITIES OF THE THIRD AGE:
THE ENGLISH VERSION

ERIC MIDWINTER

The out-and-out Chauvinist might rejoice in the United
Kingdom's version of the University of the Third Age, for it
seems to incorporate a medley of characteristics usually
deemed peculiarly English.   There is a mildly mocking air
about its use of that somewhat portentous title.   There is a
stubborn refusal to be overly theoretical about its structure.
There is a valid and stern determination to wax independent.
There is a rugged air of suspicion about the infallability of
authority.   It certainly adds up to what, on a twilit evening
and with the light behind it, might be called flexibility, but is
perhaps nearer what Anglo-Saxons are wont disarmingly to
refer to as 'muddle'.   It might, at the onset, be helpful to
tease out the meanings of these four aspects.

(A) A Portentous Title
First, as to the title.   It is, of course, an unashamed
burglary of the continental usage and reflects a genuine effort
to align the British endeavour with the international activity.
From its French beginnings some dozen years ago, the idea
has spread to several countries, although, numerically, the
emphasis remains in France, which has roughly two thirds the
world's U3A's.   The classic model is the identification of an
organised body of older students with its local university,
with, in each case, a contract negotiated with that institution
for the provision of tutorial succour.   The lesson of bargaining
for what is required, as opposed to accepting meekly what is
proferred, has not been lost on this side of the Channel, but.
in effect, precious few British U3A's rely. wholly or partly,
on institutional assistance of that kind.
     The reasons for this are mixed, even contrary.   The
situation reflects the variegated pattern of adult and continuing
education already in existence in Britain, with its mesh of

local authority, university extra-mural, Workers' Educational Association, Open University and other elements. But it also reflects the supposition that such agencies have either ignored, or are incapable of responding to, the needs of older people.

Thus, the title 'University of the Third Age' is deliberately used in two senses. On the one hand, it tries to boost the image of what should and can be provided for our older citizens. Whatever else, it is less demeaning than the labels of other services organised for that age group by the state: 'meals on wheels', 'home helps', 'day centres': these hardly have the exciting ring of colourful and mettlesome bustle. 'Third Age' is certainly a major improvement, for it avoids the wasting strictness of a chronological division. It refers to a phase of life rather than the accident of a birthday. It accepts that, after an opening 'age' of dependent childhood and education and a second 'age' of active economic and, for many, domestic and social involvement, a period follows, presaging the fourth stage of dependence and death, in which one is in fine fettle but with the major socio-economic commitments completed. It covers, then, not just the officially 'old' - the over-sixties or sixty-fives - but, for instance, the man unluckily made redundant in his fifties and with no prospect of other full-time employ; the non-working woman who has perhaps given prime years to the care of a sick relative; parents whose children have grown up and left home, and so forth. Of course, the distinction is less startlingly clearcut than with the appalling rigidity of, say, compulsory retirement on a given day, but it is, nonetheless, a genuine arc of most people's life-span.

On the other hand, there is a slight tongue-in-cheek feature about the deployment of the word 'university'. The studied inference is that the U3A is not one of your new-fangled, modern universities of the last hundred or so years, obsessed with weird epistemological divisions, with arbitrary notions of what constitutes scholarship, with a bizarre urge to grade and re-grade its clients in an atmosphere of false competitiveness, and with a fierce compulsion to maintain these mystiques for the supposed benefits of a tiny, privileged minority. The U3A, the inference continues, is of a purer, more ancient stamp. It returns to the older connotation of the early medieval university, with, in its ideal form, the concept of fellow-students joined together in the selfless pursuit of knowledge and truth for its own sake. In other words, the U3A cocks a perky snook at the conventional university, and, by implication, criticises it.

The U3A tag, has, however, caused difficulties in the public mind, and not merely among the choleric defenders of existing universities, outraged at such a cavalier use of the sacred name. The difficulties have been, as difficulties often are, the other face of the advantages. The insouciant 'university' claim has, therefore, both attracted those in search of some kind of degree or qualification, anathema to the trueblooded U3A-er, and discouraged those who expected that U3A might prove just as precious and offputting as its statutory namesake. The former have had quietly to be directed elsewhere, and the latter persuaded that the outlook was not so grim as they had mournfully visualised.

Nonetheless, several local groups, because of such factors, have decided on their own nomenclature, while preserving the general principles of U3A-ship. The acronym itself has become, like UCD or LSE before it, acceptable and accepted. At least one local branch has decided to adhere to the abbreviation without making explicit for what it stands, just as, occasionally, one cannot always recall the full version of ICI, BOC, or UNICEF. The national umbrella body for the U3A's is, for example, registered for charitable purposes as the Third Age Trust. So the title of the movement has been the subject, like many titles, of grave debate. At the same time, that means, on the positive side, that it is an ebullient talking point, and it has to be said that no preferable generic name (as opposed to some splendid parochial instances) has been suggested.

(B) A Theoretical Frailty

That lengthy log of the passions evoked by the title is a correct reflection of what has never failed to cause argument. 'Third Age' is sometimes mistaken for 'Third World', as an additional complication, and, as several have severely remarked, it is an ill-advised label which requires such an elaborate explanation. It does offer, however, a tidy introduction to the second of those English 'peculiarities'; a wholesome suspicion of too pedantic a theoretical diktat. It has been said that, if the limerick had been created on the continent, then logical, latin academics would have insisted that the Edward Lear formula would have become the unbreakable mould, with, for instance, the fifth being a reprise of the first line, and the middle third and fourth phrases as strictly governed. In less rational hands, the form has, in fact, known wild excess; thus:

> There once was a bard of Japan
> Whose verses no one could scan
> When asked why 'twas so
> He said, 'yes, I know;

> The main reason is because I try to get as many words
> into the last line as ever I possibly can'.

There would be no point denying that the U3A movement in
Britain defiantly lacks a rigid form and that, indeed, it tries
to get as many types into the running as ever it possibly can.
The proliferation of sizes, shapes and styles is sufficient to
cause some furiously to ponder whether there is any common-
alty at all. There are sizeable, quite highpowered versions;
there are tiny, aimiable instances. One may cater for a
township; another for a region. Some may have the backing of
professional and institutional big guns, where, elsewhere, two
or three individuals might be struggling to launch a U3A from
someone's home.

The rightly celebrated Cambridge U3A was the first major
enterprise, although one or two of the smaller brethren did
actually organise meetings before the Cambridge launch at the
Easter of 1982. An embryonic national committee was born at
much the same time, when there were no more than half a dozen
initiatives being contemplated, and, by the summer of 1983,
when the third of a number of national seminars was organised,
there were some thirty or forty groups, active or at an advanced
stage of planning, in the field. At that juncture, the small
committee was extended by election to seven, charitable status,
with attendant financial benefits, was offered affiliate members,
a news bulletin was planned and an annual meeting mounted.

Part 2 of this book describes, in general and by specific
case-study, the history of the movement thus far, but that
relation between centre and locality touches closely on the issue
of theoretical structure, and warrants some examination. The
two elements grew organically, and liaison between them was
largely unforced. As local bodies formed, there was a natural
desire to exchange ideas, and some kind of national clearing-
house was welcome. Speakers, advisers, newsletters and even
some small amounts of seed-money were made available centrally, with the help of the by no means excessive charitable
funds at the national committee's disposal. Press and media
coverage and appearances stimulated some public response,
in terms of potential organisers as well as putative members,
and this helped enormously. Nationally, a kit - 'U3A DIY' -
was constructed from the early experience of pioneer groups,
and this proved quite popular.

In this creakingly cyclic way, local groups grew in number
and the central body grew in strength, to the point where a
second part-time organiser, to act as a promulgator on a

countrywide basis as a complement to the present centrally based secretary and convenor, was being contemplated. A simple constitution emerged. Groups which wish to affiliate to the national league have the right to choose a representative to that central convention which, in turn, elects the national committee. In the solemn terms of the political scientist, the U3A movement is a confederation.

All of which says precisely nothing about the objectives of or criteria for membership. There is a tacit assumption, optimistic rather than naive, that groups which have contacted the central office and talked with one another know themselves whether they are U3A in character. It is hazardous. Already there has been a slightly embarrassing case of a dog-in-the-manger-ish outfit which, having collapsed itself, somehow managed to thwart temporarily a replacement venture in the same area. But it is consciously nebulous. Frankly, until groups have tried this or that technique and have learned by trial and error, it would be folly to whistle up a detailed theory of U3Agery and firmly insist that it be obeyed to the letter. Moreover, it is unlikely that so solid a structure will ever emerge, for it is already apparent, and as the case-studies in Part Two confirm, that there are many roads to Rome.

Self-evidently, a University of the Third Age is for older rather than younger persons, although, as the redundant forty year olds of the Devon branches pleasingly demonstrate, the term is comparative and not definitive. Beyond that, the primitive theory is best pronounced negatively. The U3A eschews standards of eligibility and avoids the establishment of qualifications. It maintains expenditure (not least, as its organisers would ruefully admit, through lack of choice) as low as possible, and only rarely pays tutorial salaries. It is not just about what is normally thought of as academic. Physical and recreational activities, as well as a broad gamut of intellectual pursuits, might be on offer, while, in some groups, research and the consideration of the issue of ageing in the United Kingdom are matters which are uppermost.

Perhaps the nearest approach to a theoretical pattern is to be found in the principles or guidelines included in the national committee's prospectus and which, originally, were devised by Peter Laslett, a chief founder of the movement in Britain and Chairman of the U3A in Cambridge. They run as follows:

i. The University of the Third Age shall consist of a body of persons who undertake to learn and to help others to learn. Those who teach will be encouraged also to learn and those who learn shall also teach, or in other ways assist in the functioning of the institution - by, for instance, counselling other members, offering tuition and help to the housebound, bedridden and hospitalised, by assisting in research projects, by helping to provide intellectual stimulus for the mass of the elderly in Britain, by taking part in offers of manpower to educational and cultural institutions which may require this, such as art galleries, museums, libraries and so on. Secretarial and administrative or fund raising assistance would be an important function for those wanting to help the institution.

    ii. Joining the University shall be a question of personal choice. No qualifications shall be required and no judgements made by the University of the Third Age as between applicants. The standards of the University should be those set by its individual classes and other activities, and the form taken by each individual pursuit shall be decided by members collaborating for this purpose.

    iii. The curriculum of the University of the Third Age shall be as wide as its human and financial resources permit, but the preference of members will be the only criterion of what is done. Strong emphasis will be laid on research projects, on practical skills, on physical and allied leisure activities as well as on intellectual and academic pursuits. Insistence on learning as an end in itself will guide the decisions as to what activities to undertake.

    These are the leading guidelines for the University of the Third Age, and the Committee has, in fact, agreed a more detailed format of twenty principles. Where a local group feel they can subscribe in general to those tenets, and where the national committee recognise, with equal tolerance, the group's good faith, there, then, is a U3A brought into being; for it is recognised in the scriptures that in my father's house there are many mansions.

(C) A Sturdy Independence

That broad church-ness is, in turn, a valid manifestation of the third feature under review, namely, the sturdy independence of each U3A in Britain. But that independence reflects much more than the benign refusal of the central body to impose an onerous dogma or, should it err in that officious direction, the local branches' potential to resist. The basic issue is that of self-regulation, and this independence is asserted not just of other branches or a national committee, but of other public providers. In practice, this varies substantially. Some U3A's have developed under the wing of a friendly institution, often at the bidding of an active and sympathetic tutor. Others have

Universities of the Third Age: The English Version

puritanically put temptation behind them, even to the point of refusing to seek any form of public funding. Nonetheless, the former would claim that their powers of self-determination have not been usurped, that the discreet use of accommodation and clerical support has been indispensable to the foundation of a U3A, and that a close relationship between a statutory and a voluntary agency is mutually advantageous.

It has to be confessed that there is some contentiousness on the fringes of this issue. Put extremely, there are those who believe that any connection with the existing system is damaging, at least psychologically, while their opponents insist that the current service should be revised to cope more effectively with an older clientele. All agree that the system has failed elderly people disastrously. There is no sadder wryness in British education than the onset of mass leisure at retirement leading to an abrupt collapse in the take-up of educational chances. Only a handful, certainly less than 200,000 of Britain's ten million over-sixties, are, at any given time, involved in any kind of official education activity.

The reasons for this are as well-rehearsed as they are regrettable. Highly practical points, like the costly fees, the inadequacies of public transport, the security fears about the streets after dark, rub shoulders with deeply entrenched cultural prejudices, like the fatal association in the popular mind of education with youth and its sister myth, the automatic decline of mental faculties with age. Several of these important aspects will be elaborated in proper detail in later chapters, but the institutional dimension touches closely on the initial structure of U3As. The question amounts to the degree of culpability within existing institutions for a lamentable state of affairs whereby, plainly, those enthused by the notion of providing educational nurture for older people operate more or less from a standing start; that is, they must assume that, for all practical purposes, there is scarcely any provision at all.

The optimists urge that the universities and polytechnics and the local authority adult and continuing education agencies must be forced or persuaded to mend their ways and provide more realistically for a massive age-group, massively disadvantaged. They claim that it would be foolish to turn one's back on the resources available in the huge complex of British education, resources, indeed, purchased, especially in the post-war boom years, out of the taxes and rates of the very retired people who now receive hardly a jot or tittle of that bounty.

The pessimists are much less sanguine. They argue that

9

it is the very institutionalism of the existing agencies, and not just their lack of will or imagination, which makes them faulty in this regard. They are remote and divorced from ordinary humanity, and this particularly affects the older generation, most of them who left school at thirteen or fourteen, four-fifths with no qualifications whatever, and only one in twenty of whom, compared with almost four in twenty of the younger age-groups, has had higher educational experience. Disheartened by their past schooling and discouraged by their present perception of it, the argument runs, elderly people exhibit a marked distrust of the overweening formalism and narrowness of the public sector.

The U3A national committee has adopted a pluralistic stance. It is prepared to campaign for much greater access for older citizens to the prevailing institutions. It accepts that, with more sensitive or more colourful approaches, in-takes of elders might and should be extended in traditional fields. At the same time, it places greater prominence on its own essential role as the promoter of a new style of agency. It sees no incompatibility in this. Some defenders of the established system, itself under financial and other attack, have accused U3As of further undermining the stability of the existing framework by concentrating on a novel and largely non-statutory approach. The U3A pioneers reject this charge on the grounds that there is room and need for both approaches: indeed, before the educational slack in the potential elderly market is taken up, there will need to be many more developments, some adaptive reforms of what is, some entirely fresh devices.

For it is a significant part of the U3A pitch that the scale of the question of educational provision for older people requires the invention of new institutions, of which the University of the Third Age could be the first of several. With perhaps as many as fifteen million people in the 'third age', Britain, along with most other developed nations, faces that most frightening of challenges, namely, an unprecedented one. No societies have hitherto enjoyed what should be the luxury of maybe a quarter of their populations living lengthy periods of post-work existence. Many people shedding economic and social responsibilities in their fifties may now expect to remain active and healthy for twenty or thirty years, in some cases for as long again as they have negotiated those economic and social responsibilities of the 'second age'. With no previous experience to guide us, there is an urgent need to experiment and learn briskly. A logical assumption might be that opportunities for constructive mental as well as physical activity would be socially desirable, in part to postpone and shorten the onset of the dependent and

Universities of the Third Age: The English Version

thus, from the community standpoint, excessively expensive 'fourth age'; in part as a fitting reward for the previous labours of the older generation. There is also the moral factor that, without opportunities of this kind, there is, yet again, an emphasis on the second class nature of senior citizenship. Equally, it must surely be accepted that, certainly over the next quarter century, public provision for many of the elderly population, of the type and level afforded for the present two per cent who participate, could scarcely be contemplated. It would both be too expensive and too inflexible; most older people would be unlikely to be attracted by the current institutional profferings, however deliciously packaged, and, were that to happen, the country could not afford it.

The U3A enterprise, therefore, asserts the virtue of independence as its novel contribution to the debate, and, as a corollary, adds the related virtue of frugality. In brief, there is no strong tradition for the self-regulatory principle in British education. It is not completely absent. Brave souls and bold agencies have, sometimes successfully, piloted co-operative schemes, but they have been unusual. Normalcy in the British education system has been and still is the professional dictation of the form and content of the programmes. Localised campaigns and consultations or sheer market pressures might, occasionally, lead to changes of mind, but these are rare. Because the learners, it is supposed, are too immature to decide, because of the dictates of examination pressures, because of one of a dozen other reasons, it is the custom to present programmes to the public. For those beyond the school-leaving age, it is a question of take-it-or-leave-it; for those before the school-leaving age, it is a matter of take-it.

In British education, the customer does not become a consumer until, compulsorily or voluntary, he or she has accepted the programme. It is precisely this acute absence of consumer sensitivity which has led some U3A protaganists to have nothing to do with schools and colleges and to advise seeking the aid of libraries which, they argue, are much more attuned to customer needs. The essential characteristic, then, of a U3A is that it is the creation of its members and that they make the decisions about what subjects should be taught and to what levels and in what style. Those U3As which are ostensibly under sponsorship of a traditional institution tend to adhere to that principle, and, in doing so, most clearly reflect the continental U3A practice of negotiating some form of tutorial contract with the mother agency.

On a day by day basis, the process is, obviously, a cyclic

one. A public meeting or a working party may draw up the initial schedules, and then as memberships grow in numbers and experience, the democratic regulo extends. It is difficult to overestimate the dramatic force of this change. British educational institutions are financed by the state and those controlled by local education authorities are, theoretically, at the behest of the people's representatives. But, in the humdrum sense of daily management, it is wellnigh impossible to claim for any public sector body that it is owned by its users. A progressive tutor here or there might devolve his responsibility on to his students, but, in the last analysis, they would never, like U3A members, own their institution.

In this respect, U3As are more akin to the best of pre-school play groups and mother and toddler groups, of which well over thirty thousand exist in Great Britain. Where nearest their own ideal, they are the creation of the parents whose requirements they meet. Like some U3As, they might employ the patronage, especially in the early days, of another organisation, such as a church or other local voluntary group; but, basically, they are their own creature to have and to hold. In their mild and inoffensive manner, U3As, therefore, are an illustration of the co-operative mode, closer in style, perhaps, to the Rochdale Pioneers than the University Senate.

U3As, in that regard, are part of an imposing lineage of social and economic ventures which have refused either to bow the knee to soulless public bureaucracy or open the purse for avid commercial agencies. Britain has had a colourful history of voluntary endeavour, in that connotation of being non-public and non-commercial. Its record of economic co-operatives has not been strong, but in community development, charitable work, and, probably most of all, in cultural and recreational activity (its thousands of amateur sporting and dramatic and musical societies and clubs, for instance) Britain has shown remarkable eagerness and durability. It is this tradition of collective self-help upon which U3As draw, and for which self-evidently, there is sufficient scope within the ranks of the retired. That is not to suggest that public resources, central and local, in money and in kind, would not be welcome and are not needed. There is also the tradition of public funds utilised to foster voluntary effort, and U3A protagonists have called upon the government for that kind of unstringed support.

It is a commonplace of government financing that voluntary work is superficially attractive because less costly than a wholesale public commitment. Often this means doing good on the cheap, but, in the case of the University of the Third Age,

Univerities of the Third Age: The English Version

that argument does not hold: proponents of U3As are in the
blissful position of claiming that cheaper is actually more
effective. The proposition is that the heavyweight or goldplated
character of an education service based on costly buildings and
a costly professional cadre is, in itself, offputting to many of
the likely recipients and too large and impersonal to respond to
small scale need. Thus one aspect of the frugal independence
of U3As has been to arrange for comfortable, informal surrounds
for their own sake.

An interesting sidelight on this has been the relative
difficulty of setting up U3As in larger conurbations, where those
keen to participate have perhaps been numerous but widespread.
The more successful models have tended to be rural or small
town ones with, in some cases, several sub-branches established
over a wide country area. The lesson seemed to be that, for
example, a large city would, like a shire county, require several
rather than just one U3A. Even in two or three sizeable examples,
which are operating perfectly happily, the actual locations used
may be quite numerous. American surveys have underpinned
what is now a common British impression. In New York three-
quarters of the elderly were not prepared to travel more than
five miles or for half an hour to classes and in California one
in five stated an absolute preference for home-based courses.
Implicit in much of this is the need to take the mountain to
Mahomet, and, already, lots of U3A activities are taking place
in the homes of members.

The need to recruit and formulate plans at district and
street level is uppermost. Two fairly obvious illustrations
must suffice. Some groups may follow on television a serialised
classic novel or a series of scientific programmes, much more
telling fare, incidentally, than the stilted sentences of all but
the most impressive tutors. Such groups would thereafter read
further and meet for discussion and argument, but, at that first
juncture, the person's sitting room effectively replaces the
lecture hall. Possibly more important is the case of the housebound or hospitalised older person, or the U3A member who is
perhaps temporarily ill or not extensively mobile. Several U3As
have schemes to accommodate such people by regular visits of
sympathetic co-students and other means. In those cases the
sickroom or hospital is substituted for the classroom or
laboratory.

Universities of the Third Age proclaim the existence
around us in our environment of the wherewithal for successful
educational action. The prestigious erections of the modern
system, those citadels to the belief that lavish and overt

expenditure is the key to scholarship, are, to some extent, regarded as static and narrowing. U3As provide, in the main, for those who cannot or do not wish to travel far, who wish to join together, without the stress of academic rivalry, with, usually, small numbers of their fellows, in, often times, uninhibiting and unostentatious places. We assert the right of every trueborn Englishman or Englishwoman to start, if they so desire, a university in their own back parlour. An English-man's home is, or could be, his college.

(D) An Anti-authoritarian Approach

That polemical motto leads, naturally enough, to the fourth item on this chapter's agenda: the rebellion against authority. The steadfast assertion of independence is, of course, a staging-post in that direction, but the critique, in some U3As, advances even further down the trail. Put simply, the role of the tutor has been challenged and indeed frequently abandoned. The conventional chasm between the dominant teacher and the passive learner has been bridged by the magical device of refusing to acknowledge the categories. U3As have members. Membership carries the obligation to give as well as take. Members should offer as well as accept teaching.

That stern puritanism does not, needless to say, extend to all U3A activities. If membership declares itself in favour of submission to tutorial rule, then that is their business. Another U3A might find that, unless the principle is broken, it is im-possible to find a tutor and run a course. It is worth adding, however, that, even in extremis, few U3As actually employ teachers, relying on volunteers, usually of Third Age status themselves, and regarding them as members. It equally merits note that, by eschewing the payment of salaries, U3As dodge the most burdensome expenditure suffered by the public education system, just as, in chief, they avoid the second most onerous expense, that of accommodation.

It is sometimes, of course, necessary and right for U3As to employ professional staff. These are and would be more in the nature of convenors and stewards than of didacts. Particularly in the opening phases, such organising genius may be indispensable. U3As require facilitators, men and women who will use their skills to help others form groups and encourage members to participate in a learning network. This reluctance to set the schoolmaster or mistress high on the pedantic pedestal is rare. Even those adult education bodies, such as the Workers Educational Association, which might claim for themselves an element of democratic oversight, have scarcely ever ditched the professional tutor.

The rationale is social, not economic, amiable although that secondary consideration might be. The notion is based foursquare on the assemblage of experience and skills which is the automatic gift of the Third Age. By dint of living, working, travelling, enjoying hobbies and holidays, fighting wars, raising children, a veritable treasury of knowledge is spontaneously available, and it is the task of the U3A to mobilise and channel that resource which, otherwise, would, like so many other attributes of Third Agery, be pitifully wasted.

One must first free one's mind of the restrictive practices of outworn epistemology and pedagogics. There is no limitation on the substance of U3A coursework. There is no measure on its purported value, beyond the essential willingness of the membership to listen, enjoy or otherwise absorb itself in such material. There is no inference that human communication is the exclusive talent of a small professionalised elite. Thus U3A memberships, ideally, share what content they may, with each the other.

Hackles are raised by this placid assumption that teaching is not, in some circumstances, quite the esoteric and mystical art its practitioners would have the public imagine. At one of the first public meetings in Glasgow where this principle was debated, some of that great city's dominies were mortally shocked at the contention, and labelled it 'harmful' and even 'dangerous'.

No one would claim that it is a counsel of perfectibility. The older autodidact can be boring and domineering, just as much as any professionally qualified teacher who happens to have those faults. In what are frequently small groups, it may be impossible to cover all tastes with this formula, but it has to be said that, thus far, the combined talents of these groups has occasionally offered a tastier variety of interests than some evening centres. The immediate barrier is the innate conviction of many older people, lay victims of the clerical conspiracy, that the leadership of a discussion or the exposition of an interest is totally beyond them. Two features are important, and here an adept tutorial skill may be of value. One is the insistence that the fundamental rule of sharing is adhered to, and that full participation of everyone is the prime objective: once that is determined, the teaching role loses some of its fears for those reared in the acceptance of the teacher as the sole and authoritarian contributor to the discourse. The other is a further endorsement for homely environs: a member is that much more likely to feel confident enough to adopt these roles in a friendly and unstressful situation.

Above all else, there is the recognition that the end of U3A-ship is the same as its means. It is education, in its broadest definition and for its own sake. It is an attempt to exercise the mental, cultural and social muscles of its participants, simply in order that these do not atrophy and for their continued enjoyment, pride and self-respect. It is at once the purest and the most excellent of reasons. In a nutshell, the University of the Third Age provides the intellectual equivalent of jogging.

It might be instructive to muse over a year in the life of a tiny Hertfordshire group which has confined itself fairly sternly to these perhaps daunting regulations. Its membership has been, at most, forty or fifty and it has met weekly, normally with an attendance around twenty or twenty-five. It has appointed its own officers, although, in its origins, it was dependent on external local supports, and still enjoys the inexpensive use of a small hall. The social background of its members is wide, and only some four or five have had higher educational experience. Over the year no less than fifteen of this number led a discussion or, alternately, introduced some topic, ranging from computers and the cultivation of fuschia to the electricity industry and estate management. Visits and musical sessions were also organised, and those not ready to contribute tutorially have manfully fulfilled other tasks of a secretarial or other nature.

Several points are of significant note. Several members have, gradually and under the comforting influence of a sociable milieu, volunteered to 'teach' who, originally, had been disinclined to do so. That growing self-confidence has been perhaps the most notable and pleasing development. Another feature has been the ingenious solution to the criticism that academic self-help leads to a sporadic and inconsequential programme. The fact aside that, if the members so choose, that is of no import, this particular group has sometimes adopted a fortnightly pattern, alternating a once-off session with a series, the first of which was a six-part survey of European studies under the guidance of one member. Two other such series - aspects of London's history and specific national cultures - have been planned, and in a further development, various members have accepted the task of researching into and then leading on one or other item of each of these schedules.

In such ways has the idea of the 'mutual aid' university taken root in Britain. No U3A stalwart has any jealous, possessive sentiment about the formula. Not only will it continue to vary

considerably in practice, according to the needs and predilec-
tions and conditions of each new group, it will, undoubtedly,
soon be joined by, maybe superceded by, other quite different
agencies aimed at enhancing the educational opportunities of
older people. There are, for instance, valid and respectable
suspicions that this could never be a mass movement, encomp-
assing the millions who might, over coming decades, look in
vain for an appropriate educational opening.

One hopes, then, that the University of the Third Age in
Britain will not only grow in quantity and quality, but be just
the first of a score of initiatives. Nonetheless, one might add
a final wish. The social benefits, no less than the economic
advantages, of the self-help approach do suggest that, for any
large scale breakthrough in this field, the techniques of
academic mutuality may be the necessary keys. Slowly yet
and even diffidently, U3As are visibly demonstrating that
ordinary folk, with reasonable aid and encouragement, are
altogether capable of inventing their own educational destiny,
establishing, negotiating, deciding and, eventually, teaching.
Some U3As are able proudly to boast that, unsatisfied with
merely putting the lie to the legend that older people cannot
learn, they have exhibited the capability of these citizens to
tutor-organise.

To wallow in the not always felicitous jargon of administrative doctrine, U3As are de-centralising, de-institutionalising,
and de-professionalising. Far from being a disjointed stopgap,
they already, in their nobility of principle and through the
commonsensical achievement of their pioneer endeavours, call
to account the appallingly paternalist rigidities of the public
education system at large.

In an attempt to draw attention to these pilot efforts, a two-
fold plan has been used, studying first 'the general' and then
'the particular'. In Part One - 'the general' - a notable and
distinguished cast has been recruited to look at the background
to and the development of U3As in Britain. This involves the
motivating forces for the movement in this country (Peter
Laslett), set against the original and evolving philosophy of its
European model (Michel Philibert) and the spread of the idea on
a worldwide basis (David Radcliffe). To this is added a fresh
and apposite revision of how it is thought older adults do and
should learn (Paula Allman), together with an account of those
two cross-currents of thought influencing the U3A phenomenon,
community education (John Rennie) and the self-help ideal
(Michael Young).

Part Two - 'the particular' - presents case-studies of

actual U3As at work. They are preceded by a description of
the history and present incidence of U3A groups in Britain
(Dianne Norton). Four representative units, showing the
variety as well as the practical application of the idea, have
been selected: Cambridge (Vernon Futerman); Devon (Frank
Watson); Saffron Walden (John Jones and Joyce MacElroy),
and the Lancaster District (Keith Percy). This combine of
the importantly analytical and the necessarily practical will,
it is hoped provide a balanced portrait of this newest of
Britain's education developments.

Variety is indeed the spice of U3A life. As chapter seven so
clearly shows, there are as many U3A structures as there are
branches, each of them at one or another of half a dozen stages
of development, and many of them rejoicing in their own local
brand-name. There is the widespreading grandeur of the
Cambridge U3A concept; there is the many-faceted and many-
headed approach of Devon; there is the smallscale group organisation of Saffron Walden; and there is the excellent Lancaster
activity, with its valuable support from the university and from
the Manpower Services Commission.

If any prototype is emerging, it seems to be around the focus
of relatively medium-sized pockets of population. The successfully launched London U3A, while metropolitan in its catchment,
is organised on a multi-centre basis, and the Devon Third Age
Project also operates from a series of bases. There are
several groups in the Yorkshire area, but they, while inter-
connected for some purposes, individually serve given locales.
There is some evidence - Norwich, Manchester - that the larger
conurbations are not too keenly susceptible to the blandishments
of the U3A idea. Apart from the majestic and perhaps rather
special progress of Cambridge, there has developed a tendency
for the singly-based branches to settle down around, in terms of
membership, the twenty-five to a hundred mark.

A membership of this kind seems to allow for either a weekly
session for all or, perhaps coupled with this, a number of small
cells, sometimes only fours, fives and sixes of members, for
particular pursuits, often taking place in people's own homes.
This sort of membership allows for some spread of activity and
some flexibility of purpose, whilst never risking the end of that
aimiable informality and lack of imposing administrative
apparatus which so pleases many of the members.

A glance at the geographical locations of the now over fifty -
in varied states of evolution - U3As in Britain would tend to under-
score this finding. There does seem to be, in the best sense of
the term, a hometown ring about the character of U3As, with

branches starting in market-towns, in the smaller industrial townships, in rural centres and in what are sometimes called the 'villages' within the larger urban areas. Of course, as has been mentioned, the difficulties of travel and mobility play a part, but there does seem, if only, so far, impressionistically, a more positive aspect.

There does appear to be a sense of satisfaction in an identification with a district or locality which, in common or garden terms, retains a shape and a size of human proportions, and the persistent success of local history as an activity in many U3As seems to add to this feeling. That is by no means a scientific observation, but it does suggest that these 'mutual aid universities' may be meeting more needs than the desire to socialise and pursue educational activities.

Finally, it must be stressed that these are novel phenomena, and experience is, as yet, limited. Nonetheless, it cannot be denied that British U3As have crowded a rich experience into a couple of very busy years.

Chapter 2

THE EDUCATION OF THE ELDERLY IN BRITAIN

PETER LASLETT

Peter Laslett is Director of the Cambridge Group for the
History of Population and Social Structure, and in celebrated
books, like The World We Have Lost, he has won international fame for his insight into demographic issues, in
particular with regard to elderly people. A Fellow of
Trinity College, Cambridge and an expert on John Locke,
he was a founding father of the Open University and is now
Chairman of the University of the Third Age in Cambridge.

In 1980, Peter Laslett issued a report, partly financed by
the Elmhirst Trust, entitled The Education of the Elderly
in Britain, which incorporated, by way of introduction,
An Educational Charter for the Elderly (first published in
New Society, 13 March 1980). In effect, the whole course
of educational provision and the elderly in Britain stems
from this seminal study. Peter Laslett has revised,
amended and updated that report as a major contribution
to this book. Drawing on European experience and on his
own involvement with the beginnings of the Open University,
Peter Laslett trenchantly defines the educational needs of
older people and insists on their right to such provision.
His proposed solutions to the educational challenge of
providing decently for elderly people are wide-ranging, not
least in his imaginative proposals for the use of distance
teaching. The University of the Third Age, English-style,
is but one aspect of this broad conspectus, but, needless to
say, it is a significant one, and one which only makes complete
sense when set against this overall frame of reference.

(A) An Educational charter for the elderly in Britain
The facts about the educational position of the elderly in our
country are not in dispute. The British over 60 are the worst
instructed people not only in our own population, but also among
the advanced western countries as a whole. They are the least

educated community of native English speakers. This follows
from the fact that the number of years of compulsory schooling
in Britain in the 1920s was less than in the United States,
Canada, Australia or New Zealand. Opportunities for subsequent
instruction have been fewer also, at least if admission to
universities and other institutions is considered rather than
'extra mural' activities. It is not clear that French or Italian
children left school much earlier than British children in the
1920s and 1930s and countries like Portugal are clearly in a
worse position than we are in the 1980s. But, if somewhat
exaggerated, the statement draws attention to the restrictions
on educational opportunity at times when Britain was able to
afford more, sometimes much more, in the way of education
to its population of all ages than other Western countries. In
spite of this fact, the British over these years seemed satisfied
that theirs was a superior educational system, especially in
respect of the educational opportunities for adults.

Yet it could be argued that in so far as education is for life
in general, for diversion, for leisure, or for 'civilisation' as
it was once called, the older person needs educating now more
than any other one of us needs it. The fact is, however, that
the number of elderly students in classes open to them - and
these are considerable, even though supply is tiny in proportion
to need - is at the moment falling fast. This is the inevitable
outcome when fees are being forced up by a 'realistic' financial
policy, and when the educational rights of the elderly are never
mentioned. For they have got to be explicitly set down.

The elderly in the British population are proportionately
very numerous, and not likely to decrease. Nearly everyone
who reads this can reckon that he or she will one day join their
ranks. The demographers estimate that for the rest of this
century getting on for a fifth of our whole population will be over
60, elderly that is to say, with those over 70 and over 80 forming
an increasing proportion. After 2000 A.D. the total of the
elderly might rise to a quarter, or even more. At all relevant
times women will predominate over men amongst elderly persons,
quite noticeably at 60, markedly at 70 and pronouncedly at 80
and over. But men have in our day nearly all ceased working
by the age of 65. We have nine million British pensioners of
no occupation.

This charter, therefore, is intended as a charter for all
British persons, as they are now, or as they will finally be.
It consists of five educational <u>rights</u>. The right to a fair share
of the educational budget of the nation: the right to the abandonment of the identification of education with youth: the right of

access to all educational institutions on their own terms; the right to a 'distance teaching' organisation, to bring education for the elderly into the home: and the right to recognition of their unique intellectual and cultural value.

i. <u>A fair share of the budget</u>

The share of the education budget for the elderly should be fair in terms of need, and fair in terms of contributions made to the national wealth, both in the past and in the present. That need is clearly substantial, and has three distinguishable elements.

The first is for instruction itself - the relief of ignorance and all that goes with ignorance in the way of low self-esteem and lower social esteem, together with the incapacity to use existing services and opportunities.

The second is for specialized knowledge - for research undertaken in order to discover what older people most need to know, and how to make that knowledge available to them. This is especially necessary for the working class elderly, who in the 1910s, 1920s and 1930s were wretchedly prepared for life.

The third element is more difficult to define. It consists in the necessity that members of the population at large should themselves know about ageing. The elderly are entitled to assume that all citizens should recognize that they belong to one of the oldest populations which has ever existed and one which has fewer resources than many or most other similarly placed western industrial countries.

A 'fair' share will have to be defined, after discussion. It presents an intricate problem in social and political ethics, particularly as it involves the past in relation to the present. How are we to assess the justice of our having almost doubled the national expenditure on education over the last thirty years, and yet allotted virtually none of the new resources to those who are now elderly? It was they, after all, who created the wealth which made it possible for us to expand the educational system at all. Public funds for universities were doubled between the mid-sixties and the mid-seventies. These are just the institutions which do least, and perhaps can do very little, to educate the mass elderly. Their function in any programme of the kind we are concerned with would be for the most part confined to adding further to the knowledge of their own pre-dominantly middle-class graduates in their later years, confirming and intensifying the disparity over the life course.

The elderly, then, cannot be said to be claiming a privileged position. In reckoning their fair educational share, account will have to be taken of the heavy demands which they can make on the more and more restricted welfare resources

of the country (for pensions, for health services, and so on).
But the elderly have never previously been thought to have
specifically educational needs at all, let alone rights.

The exercise of these educational rights might reduce the
demands of the aged for care - care which is so very costly,
especially when it is institutional. It is reasonable to suppose
that the better informed, active and interested the elderly
become, the less help of this kind they will need. The
programme which this charter may imply is not expensive in
relation to the financial and social costs of the elderly today.
It might indeed save us resources of both kinds.

   ii. Education isn't just for youth

The claim that education should not be identified only with youth
is straightforward enough, and is being increasingly recognised,
if in a rather grudging and contorted fashion. The lingering
reluctance to part with the notion that education begins at a
particular stage of early life (say five years old) and ends for
most people a dozen years later - for some of us 15 or 20 years
later - is revealed by the extraordinary vocabulary which is
being developed about education over the life course. We have
'primary' and 'secondary' education, and 'lower' and 'higher'
education. We have 'further' education and 'adult' education.
We now have still heavier officialese expressions, like
'continuing' education - even 'post-compulsory' education,
surely the prize exhibit in this collection of half-hearted
verbiage. Half-hearted because of our rather puzzling
unwillingness to recognize the fact that education is a lifelong
interchange between those who _do_ know, and can, and those who
need to know, and be able. The process begins at birth and ends
with death; or it should do. There is no social differentiation
between each educational 'stage'; only predominantly technical
differences.

The recent exercises in literacy and numeracy for the
population at large have demonstrated that it is simply not true
that all persons acquire what we think of as basic knowledge or
skill when very young or young. They may need to be taught
them at any time in their lives. They have as much right to
such teaching at 35 or 45 years old as they have at five.

This is how it goes for the updating of professional knowledge,
too. Who now believes that a doctor or an electrician, or even
an undertaker or a builder's foreman, can be taught all that he
has to know for the rest of his life by the time he reaches the
age of 25? And who, therefore, believes that all we need to know
to live as old people can be instilled into us 40 or 50 years before
we reach that stage of life?

iii. Access to all institutions

Access by the elderly to all educational institutions on their own terms must accompany the right to the abandonment of the identification of education with youth. There are discussable limits to such a right: limits of commonsense as well as of resources. Little is to be gained by trying to teach women and men in their seventies in schools where the furniture has been specially made for infants. But when we come to consider the exclusion of the elderly, especially the retired elderly, from the places where adolescents are now instructed - polytechnics or colleges of education or universities - we begin to see the substance of this claim.

Why should the community maintain all these establishments all the year round, keep them empty for almost half the time (at least in the case of universities), and yet deny access to everyone except those who happen to be current students registered as belonging to the institutions concerned? How far are their occupants justified in claiming such exclusive use, on the grounds that teaching makes it necessary? What about the playing fields and other recreational facilities they enjoy in such plenty? Why shouldn't these be open to the elderly whose leisure needs are so much greater than the young, and who are known to have a particular interest in physical exercise to keep them active? Should the universities and colleges be permitted to fill up their premises with well-heeled conference attenders during vacation, and keep old people out?

There was, in fact, an effort to introduce into Britain an American scheme for giving older people more access to university campuses. After some exploratory meetings the attempt to organise the reception of elderly persons into courses run for them by Universities and other 'higher' educational bodies was given up. No charitable body could be found which was willing to finance the essential central office to arrange for teaching to be given and to do the booking, and the plan was not strongly favoured by University Extra Mural Boards and other bodies which might have furthered the plan. It could be said that the fast growing number of organizations identifying themselves as Universities of the Third Age, or something similar, now form some sort of substitute. But few classes of this kind are yet taught by the regular staff of Universities, Polytechnics and so on. The principle of successive visitation, where elderly learners go to University at their choice, and most or finally all relevant institutions in the country are caught up in this scheme, has been lost sight of for the time. It is to be hoped that the notion will be revived in Britain, where

members of the Elderhostel Movement from the United States
are already being received on to British campuses.

These are issues which are likely to come urgent in any
case, and for several reasons. Institutions of 'higher'
education might welcome older students into their courses to
keep up numbers and to justify their existence and their
income. But a question remains whether our universities and
colleges will teach students in later life what they need, rather
than what people of undergraduate age are usually treated to.
This is why the phrase, 'on their own terms', has to be included
in a statement of this educational right of the elderly. They
may need to protect themselves against the examination
system, for example.

iv. National 'distance teaching'

The right to a national 'distance teaching' organization for the
elderly is the only one in the list which would require institutional innovation. The elderly, if less occupied than the rest
of us, are also less mobile, and have as much right to be
instructed in their own homes as the scholars of the Open
University. Indeed, should the Open University itself undertake
the task? The answer, as I see it, must be a resounding no.

This is both because the Open University is large enough
already, and because it is a university. A university is
emphatically what is not wanted by the elderly - the British
elderly as they are now, anyway. This statement may read
oddly in 1984 coming from one who has been active in starting
British Universities of the Third Age. But it should become
plain as the chapter continues that it is not inconsistent with
the view there set out. This view is that the Universities of
the Third Age are an attainable aim for those with the
educational background which is required, and for some others
too. For the mass elderly such organizations are entirely
insufficient, and, for the reasons outlined above, even a
liability. To expect of a movement which can find, and is
finding, Universities of the Third Age a remedy for the larger
problem of the educational simulation of the mass of the
British elderly is unrealistic. The idea of a university is
much overloaded. The model it stands for is badly suited to
our national social needs. By the third right, older people
would have access to the universities in any case; and some
of them have certainly exercised it already, with the Open
University and in other ways.

The issues multiply themselves under this heading, as with
everything to do with the education of the elderly. Here are
some of the questions which have to be faced:

The Education of the Elderly in Britain

Is it not wrong to make the elderly a special group - a ghetto is the word often used? This expression and implied criticism of any movement for the specific education of the elderly has been common since 1980. Those who voice it should perhaps be reminded that education has been a youth ghetto for nearly all of its history, and is only now beginning to show some responsibilities towards those not young, as bureaucracy defines youth. No one seems to object to young people having agebased institutes, educational or otherwise. Why should they be treated differently from other persons enforcedly at leisure in our society, the unemployed, for example? Then there is the question of the drawbacks of teaching at home, for the elderly stand in need of outside company. Those most in need of instruction are also those most in need of joining others of different ages to take part in co-operative activities.

There are also open questions about how much we yet possess in the way of information as to how distance teaching might work. Does anyone know what the curriculum of an 'open learning' institution would be, when it is not a university, not a college of higher education, not a polytechnic? Will people not motivated as highly as most Open University students benefit from teaching brought to them in the home? How would a potential student body be affected by its consisting predominantly of elderly women?

New knowledge is needed to respond to such questions as these, but it is likely that a mixture of 'distance learning' and in-house instruction is the most likely to be adopted. Teaching-at-a-distance - by correspondence and/or the mass media - has great attraction as a means of instruction for the elderly. A proportion of them is being cared for in hospitals or residential homes; even more are almost immobile. It is difficult to see how many of these people could otherwise be reached at all, at a price we could afford.

v. Cultural recognition

The fifth and last educational right of the old is the recognition of their cultural and intellectual importance. The Cambridge-shire College of Arts and Technology, under pressure of the cuts being imposed everywhere, recently announced its decision to cease offering the classics after the retirement of the present teacher. At least a quarter of the students in the classes were elderly people, and this proportion was growing.

Not many want the classics even in Cambridge, of course. But with the business of learning enough to earn a living as pressing as it now is, and with the numbers in what might be

called subjects of cultivation getting less - who else is at
liberty to pursue them but the leisured aged?

The last thing I wish to be understood as saying is that
many old people should want to learn Latin or Greek, or feel
inadequate if they have no desire for such a thing. Art,
archaeology, social history and family history (which includes
the history of ageing) are rather different. They come more
easily.

We are still largely ignorant of what the elderly should be
taught, or teach themselves, in order to give them that mental
stimulation which they so much need and which may go some
way towards keeping them from becoming expensive liabilities
to the health and social services. But I believe that their
ripeness, experience and wisdom fit them for a function of which
we stand pre-eminently in need - the preservation and intensi-
fication of our cultural heritage. They have a right to exercise
that function, and that right corresponds to our common need.

(B) Education and Elderly People
This educational charter for the elderly in Britain was composed
in the knowledge that their needs and rights were better recognized and provided for elsewhere. But it was drawn up before
any attempt had been made at a personal acquaintanceship with
the provision made in those other countries where the elderly
formed a considerable part of the population. It has to be
recognized that most of these countries are in the rich,
developed part of the world; at the present time it is there that
the ageing of the population has proceeded to its greatest extent,
especially in Western Europe.

Extensive experience in the university system of the U.S.A.,
which is much more widespread in its scope and purposes than
that of Britain, and also a provider of social services on a
large scale, in spite of its flavour of private enterprise, had
made it clear that those in the higher age ranges in America
were far better off than in Britain. This was primarily due to
the fact that the American elderly had received so much more
instruction in their youth, which is also true of the elderly in
the other relevant countries, but it was also owing to the fact
that the American universities had offered their graduates
refresher courses and a degree of access to their facilities not
usual in Britain.

To this extent, as is implied in the charter, the education
of the elderly is particularly a British problem. Nevertheless,
all our neighbours in Western Europe and some in Central
and Eastern Europe are, or shortly will be, in a similar

The Education of the Elderly in Britain

demographic position and, as was to be expected, it is the
Scandinavians who have most to offer to those interested in the
elderly. Not only do these countries have a long tradition of
social service of this kind, but they are now also amongst those
best able to afford the expense of such programmes. After
learning during 1979 about the Elderhostel movement of the U.S.A
an experience which brought home the urgency of getting something of the same kind going in Britain, it was decided to visit
Scandinavia, as well as Germany, later in that year. It was
particularly important to go to France, in order to pay a visit
to one of the wellknown Universités du Troisième Age. A
journey to Denmark, Norway, Sweden and Germany was
accordingly undertaken in September, with some assistance
from the Elmhirst Trust, and a visit paid to France in October.

It would be wrong to give the impression that we have been
unaware of the issue of educating the elderly in Britain, or that
nothing has been done about it. Those responsible for adult
education (the W.E.A., the Extra Mural boards and so on) have
recognized the progressive ageing of their constituents and
have modified policies to some extent in response. Those
responsible in industry and business for the retirement of
working people have founded the Pre-Retirement Association,
which instructs increasing numbers of those in their late 50s
and early 60s, mostly in the larger establishments. There has
also been some theoretical discussion and writing about the
subject.

In British universities and research centres work is going
forward in the study of ageing and the aged themselves mainly
amongst biologists and psychologists. But it has to be said that
there has been very little research so far amongst social
scientist, and almost no participation whatever on the part of
political scientists, historians, philosophers or those in the
humanities. The British effort has so far been small in relation
to that made in other comparable countries and tiny when the
extent of the elderly population is considered, and when it is
compared with research activity in other fields. No national
institute exists for the purpose to parallel that in the U.S.

There is a professional association for the social study of
ageing, the British Society of Gerontology, but it is still relatively
small, if expanding fast, and certainly small by comparison with
the organisations catering for medical and physiological
practitioners and investigators. The fact that what is sometimes called the medical model of ageing is widely seen to be
inadequate when it comes to issues of a social, cultural and
educational kind, makes this the more unfortunate. A British

initiative is long overdue, and it is good to be able to say that
there are signs that it is now under way, such as the successful
launch in 1981 of the journal Ageing and Society, edited by
Malcolm Johnson.

Nomenclature is of some importance to this topic, because
all words and expressions to do with the higher age groups have
discouraging, even demeaning associations. What is more,
ageing is not exclusively to do with the age ranges in question,
but applies to all individuals, who are ageing from birth and
show signs of physiological senescence from the middle 20s.
The fact that to call anyone old, or even retired, or elderly,
is widely felt to be uncomplimentary or worse, has led to a
series of euphemisms, of which the most used in Britain is the
American expression 'Senior Citizen'. Like all such attempts
at an evasive vocabulary of a quasi-complimentary kind, the
phrase itself has lost much or all of its virtue. A better
expression is needed which avoids euphemism, and we have
adopted the French notion of the Third Age. This nomenclature
provides the basis for the general approach which is characteristic of les Universités du Troisième Age - the third age
universities. The object of educational policy, at all levels of
education and information, and for every year of a person's
life, is to prevent an individual ever passing from the Third to
the Fourth age, a transition which for the majority need never
occur at all before final illness.

There are signs that the expression Third Age had itself
come to be looked upon in France as a little tarnished which is
somewhat discouraging. It is obviously not possible nor is it
desirable to rid the higher ages of all their associations with
physical decline and death. But the Third Age, being simply
numerical, is more objective than its rivals and an attractive
usage in itself. It will be noticed that it contains a similar
idea to that embodied in the phrases used by American
gerontologists to make the distinction between the old old and
the young old. This is a clumsier phraseology and one which
does not bear the inference that the final and unwanted stage
is by no means inevitable for all.

As for the general approach to the subject of the educational
stimulus of the elderly, four principles may be set down. They
seem to follow from the educational charter which has been set
out, and from what it is possible to learn about what may happen
if the rights in the charter are acted upon.

First principle: that a number of assumptions about the
functions of education and the duties of educators get in the
way of policy making. Since the elderly need no qualifications,

have no careers to pursue, and are not in a position to earn more by taking instruction, all talk of entrance barriers or tests of progress or examinations of any kind is largely irrel-vant to their education. In this way the educational stimulus of the aged requires an outlook different in principle from that appropriate to education as it has usually been pursued.

Even when education for retirement is at issue, instruction of the traditional kind is not required, since subsequent performance hardly matters, or rather matters in a way very different from what it does in schools and colleges. The elderly person unaware of the process of ageing, unable to cope with the social services or with the reduced circumstances imposed by society on the old, is certainly at a personal disadvantage, and this disadvantage is to some extent remediable. Everyone benefits if this handicap is overcome, society at large as well as the elderly themselves.

But this is very different from preparing a young person for life, or retraining a middle-aged person in mid-career. As for education or instruction for leisure, for the absence of an occupation of a subsistence-earning kind, this as two distinct connotations, which are difficult to reconcile with each other. In the first place it is surely a general object of all education to enrich experience. This is in no way specific to preparing the elderly for leisure, or should not be. But in the second place education is leisure, or can be said to be an important aspect of leisure. For in its literal meaning education is the drawing forth of a person's capacities for experience and fulfilment.

The pre-retirement course is, therefore, inadequate or even inappropriate as education for leisure. Such an undertaking, if it is possible at all, would have to go on throughout the rest of the life of the person retiring. Once this is recognized, it is easy to see the force of the argument of those radicals who maintain that pre-retirement education is only an expedient of a society unable to find work for all of its active citizens to reconcile them to being idle.

Second principle: that the traditional framework of 'levels' in British education is unsuited to the educational stimulus of the elderly. It makes little sense to think of the elderly being educated at university level, or at sixth form level, or of their being unable to keep up a higher educational standard. It makes no sense at all to think of such a pupil climbing from one level to another. It may be important to young people engaged in mastering a difficult technique that they be protected from the entry into their classes of elderly persons in no position to do as well as they do. But this is an argument in favour of the separate educational treatment of the old, and does not imply that standards should be applied to them.

Third principle: that the social status hierarchy of British educational institutions is an obstacle to the adoption of a proper policy. The associations which go with university teaching in our country are particularly unfortunate because we have had an elitist university tradition to a greater degree than any of the other countries with which I am familiar. Because this is so, the very title 'extra mural' has unwelcome implications: even the WEA and the polytechnics have not so far succeeded in resisting the capillary action of elitism on all English educational institutions. Every effort has to be made to prevent the education of the elderly from going up market in this way, which argues for the importance of an entirely fresh start.

There is a difficulty here, however. It would be a pity, it would be a palpable loss to the education of the elderly, if the motive of intellectual and even social emulation disappeared altogether. That this motive can be effective is illustrated by the success of the Open University. Policy makers have to tread carefully in this area.

An implication of the three principles so far laid down is that there is a sharp divide between a policy appropriate to those, a tiny minority in Britain, who have developed 'higher educational' or 'university' aspirations, and all the rest. For the most part, though not entirely, the division arises because of previous educational experience and it is this which makes for a pronouncedly unequal division in Britain between what one might call the interested, motivated middle-class elderly and the uninterested mass of the elderly. Policy for these two very unequal parts has to be very different. It is of the greatest importance that what works for the middle-class minority shall not be assumed to be appropriate for the great majority, and above all that a watered down version of what is offered to the one shall not be thought to serve for the other. It must never be forgotten that the universities are upper-class elitist institutions in the eyes of the British working-class woman or man, and that all competitively based education rejects the unsuccessful, who resent it more or less, and for longer and shorter periods of their lives.

A realistic assumption of the educator of the elderly is that every one of his subjects has been made to feel this rejection, or has had so little contact with education since his childhood that education means almost nothing to him or to her.

The Education of the Elderly in Britain

Fourth principle: that the educational stimulus of the elderly
is, from the pupil's point of view, urgent in a way which is quite
different from the urgency of education of other kinds. It is a
novel and rather frightening fact about a contemporary population
like our own that nearly all the deaths occur to those over 60.
Though it may seem, with $21\frac{1}{2}$ years to live for women at that
age, and 18 for men, that there is a surprising amount of time
during which people are going to live when elderly or old, it
must not be overlooked that numbers are diminishing rapidly
at all relevant ages and very rapidly at the later ones. In this
crucial respect the elderly are entirely different both from the
school population and those in adult education. This is literally
their last chance and anything done to help them has to be done
very fast. It is now intended to study the educational needs of
the elderly, from the viewpoint of the two major groups, the
'interested' minority and the 'uninterested' majority.

(C) Educational stimulus of the interested middle-class elderly
There are very many ways in which the interested middle-class
elderly are being educated at the present time in other countries,
but it is convenient to class them as of three types: education
within the established universities; founding university-type
institutions for the elderly, run by the elderly: providing for
the elderly in adult education programmes, along with others.
In my view the second of these is most effective.
    We have tentatively begun to found in Britain Universities
of the Third Age, and we shall continue to do so. We should
here follow the French initiative, though we should not confine
the interested middle-class elderly to these institutions. We
should, furthermore, make an attempt to use those who come
together to learn in our Universities of the Third Age as
instructors for the mass of the aged, who constitute the real
problem.

Admitting the elderly to regular university courses
In all the countries visited, the elderly are admitted to the
regular universities and higher educational institutions, in
larger or smaller numbers. In Britain least is done, and
universities tend only to admit elderly people who satisfy the
'entrance standards' imposed on their juniors. There are,
nevertheless, some students over 60 even at Cambridge colleges.
In Scandinavia the elderly have a right to attend universities
without satisfying the requirements imposed on school-leavers,
and they do so, though on a restricted scale. Recent educational
reform movements in these countries, especially in Denmark

and Sweden, have insisted on these rights, in Sweden as part
of the compensatory policy which attempts to make up to the
old for what they have missed because higher education was on
a much smaller scale when they were of an age to receive it.

In the charter for the elderly this right is insisted on for
British citizens, and reference is made to the issue of justice
between the age groups which lies behind the claim. It is
important that this right be formally secured for our elderly,
and, in 1983 the Forum for the Right of the Elderly People to
Education adopted the principle that no educational institution
in Britain which did not admit elderly persons as of right to
instruction should be given money from the state. But, in my
judgement, the admission of the elderly without entrance
examination to the ordinary courses which exist at institutions
of 'higher education' will not accomplish much. It should happen.
It would do good symbolically. It will benefit some individuals.
But nothing else seems likely to come of it.

The changed age structure of the population of Western
European countries makes it important that all possible
education patterns for the elderly should be explored, even for
the small minority of the interested middle-class elderly. The
outcome of experimental ventures, in Scandinavia and elsewhere,
may well be instructive, but, as things are at present, it seems
that the University of the Third Age, an autonomous second
university run for and largely by the elderly themselves within
an existing 'regional academy' is the most promising expedient
in the long term.

L'université du troisième age - The University of the Third Age
What we need to do is to foster a sense of general educational
responsibility in British Universities, to the population as a
whole, to the elderly population in particular, as well as to their
localities. The organization of education in France fosters such
a sense of responsibility by grouping of the higher educational
institutions of a region into an academy, as for example
L'académie de Basse Normandie. L'université du 3me age de
Basse Normandie is located in the city of Caen on the campus
of the University of Caen, which is the major institution of
l'Académie, and, although it shares the buildings of that
regular University, the Third Age University is an institution
of its own, run to a large extent by its own elderly students.
Although no British U3A has adopted the Caen model - in Britain
actual ownership of the agency resides in the elderly membership, unlike in France where the elderly do not really own their
institution - its advantages are worth noting.

i.   Low cost.   The pupils Caen pay only Frs. 75. (about £9) per
course per year, and this is the regular university year from
October to May.   In September 1978, the third year of the
institution's existence, when the number of pupils was 514, the
budget was Frs. 147, 233 (about £15,000).   It should be noted,
incidentally, that the 514 students had risen from 440 (139 males,
301 females) in 1976/7, and rose to 567 in 1978/9.   The £15,000
does not include the salaries of the university teachers who are
employed by the regular University of Caen.   But it is noteworthy
that £4,500 was raised by fees paid by students, the rest
coming from the municipal contributions and from banks, etc.
Though there was a deficit in the year reported on, it seems
clear that new resources are being tapped and existing facilities
more intensively used.
ii.   The elderly get what they want.   This seems to be mainly
languages (34% of the syllabus) but includes quite a range of other
things; physical education 10%, literature 9%, geology 7%,
history 7%, arts 6%, 'design' 6%, etc.   Many of the meetings
or teaching occasions are lectures, passively attended, or
visites, mostly what we should think of as guided tours led by
a teacher.
iii.   Participation in research.   In the case of Caen the major
research project was organised by the biologists in the university
interested in the fauna of the Normandy beaches, crustacea,
which the elderly students were systematically reporting upon.
This type of collaborative research, where a number of
interested but unskilled people in the localities supply uniform
information to a band of full-time researchers, has great
promise for the educational stimulus of the elderly.   We have
used it extensively, though not specifically with elderly people,
at the Cambridge Group for the History of Population and Social
Structure, where the largest national archive which yet exists
for historical demography has been built up by this means.
The sense of taking part in a worthwhile academic exercise and
systematically contributing to knowledge is a great addition to
the studies of the volunteers.   It is a method already adopted
by one or two British U3As.
iv.   The organisation proliferates easily.   At Caen branch units,
antennes, have grown up rapidly in the lower Norman town, once
more being set up on the initiative of the elderly people, and
this expedient for extending the activity to rural areas could be
of importance in Britain.
v.   The possibility of a teaching force to help with the educational stimulation of the mass.   If it should turn out to be the
case that the great difficulty of implementing a programme of

mass education for the elderly in Britain would be lack of
organisers and teachers, then the volunteer students in the
Universities of the Third Age might perhaps supply the need.
It has to be said that no such attempt has been made in France,
where it could be stated that the Universities of the Third Age
are run by middle-class people, for middle-class people and
middle-class purposes.

There are obvious limitations to the Universities of the Third
Age in their present form. They exist in France because of an
excess of teaching capacity in the established universities, an
excess which already exists indeed in England and will rise as
the 'regular' student body contracts. But if the movement
should grow to any size, extra teaching strength would have to
be found and this would at once raise the cost considerably.
The Caen organisation requires mobility on the part of the
students, who have to attend away from their homes and to
provide their own transport, and it seems that every member of
L'université du Troisième Age de Basse Normandie has access
to a car. In Britain plans are already afoot in some U3As to
transcend this limitation by taking provision to the housebound
and immobilised.

In spite of these and other limitations the French are very
proud of this achievement and only too anxious to export it.

Adult Education Classes and the Interested Elderly

Under this heading is intended all descriptions of education,
other than that meted out in schools, colleges, polytechnics and
universities, to their full-time students. The enrolment of the
elderly in such classes is extensive in all the countries I have
visited, though I know of no source from which these numbers
can be estimated, certainly in our own country. It is generally
agreed, however, as we shall see, that though large numbers
of elderly people take classes, they are only a negligible
proportion of all elderly people nevertheless.

This form of educational stimulus of the interested, mainly
middle-class elderly, will obviously continue whatever
innovations take place in the field, and no move should be made
to discourage such attendance. On the contrary it is to be
hoped that a new initiative would tend to raise their numbers.
The great advantage of such teaching is that the elderly are
taken outside their homes and brought into classes alongside of
other members of the community. In the case of some of the
organisations concerned, especially in the WEA, a conscious
effort is made to prevent the student body from becoming
exclusively composed of interested middle-class pupils.

Nevertheless, the view that all that might now be needed is the expansion of conventional provision of this kind to take in more and more of the population, and particularly more and more of the elderly, is not acceptable as an adequate response to our dilemma. It is perhaps worth while listing one by one the reasons for this negative attitude.

In the first place, there are differences in the requirements of elderly people in matters of curriculum, some of them presumably arising from the singularity in their sex ratio as well as in their age. The preferences exercised by the elderly at Caen, with a strong insistence on linguistic subjects, may not be typical for France and not applicable for England. But they demonstrate that the elderly themselves do have their specific tastes which are not necessarily identical with those of younger people, and should not be foisted upon those younger people either. Perhaps a more important point is the demand amongst the elderly for physical exercise and for travel. The teaching visit to a historical building or an archaeological site seems to be of great interest to them, precisely the stimulus which is being sought.

In the second place, the times at which elderly people can attend differ, because they are far more often at liberty in what are called working hours. They can take consecutive days off for course purposes and some of them are clearly prepared to do so.

In the third place, the teaching attitude, assumptions and so on are also different, as has already been suggested in earlier sections.

In the fourth place, quite apart from the issue of curriculum, it is questionable whether the interests of younger people would be properly served if the interested elderly were to be represented in these classes in numbers proportionate to their strength in the constituency, the constituency being those able and willing to attend. The really successful recruitment of the elderly might swamp their juniors and leave little scope for the 'progressive' teaching which younger people clearly frequently need and insist upon.

In the fifth place, there is great advantage in a new start, especially one marked by institutional innovation and novelty in methods of teaching. Universities of the Third Age and distance teaching would be of this character.

In the sixth place, the classes of the kind now established could not be used to train a teaching body to tackle the problem of the educational stimulation of the mass of the elderly. If this difficult task is to be done, institutions for teaching a

particular description of middle-class elderly pupils will have
to be set up in any case.

These six considerations convince me that present educational provisions in Britain must be pronounced insufficient for
our purposes. To this it might perhaps be replied that the Open
University could be adapted and extended so as to involve the new
functions which have been described. The Open University does,
of course, teach a number of the elderly, at the higher level,as
has been said, and clearly could, if it wished, institute courses
directed particularly to them. If what has been said about the
assumptions of traditional education are true, however, this
would imply that the Open University would have to include two
very different teaching traditions and practices. The OU, is,
moreover, large enough already, as is insisted in our educational
charter, and it suffers, as no doubt all distance teaching
institutions are bound to suffer, from a heavy burden of administration. There is a further point, that the teaching of the OU
requires good sight and advanced reading skills on the part of
its pupils.

If existing institutions, including the OU, could not in
principle be extended so as to satisfy the needs we are discussing, it does not follow that younger persons should be excluded
from teaching programmes established with the elderly in mind.
Most French Universities of the Third Age take pupils of age 55
and above only, but this does not seem to me to be a necessary
limitation. What does seem to be important is that the leadership and administration of such institutions, should be in the
hands of those judged to be in the third age.

Nevertheless, one important point must be decided. Should
it become necessary in Britain to make particular provision for
the instruction of the technologically unemployed, it must surely
be done quite separately from any provision for the education of
the elderly. Retraining may stimulate intellectually, but its
proper object is decidedly not intellectual stimulation. It is an
interesting fact that the elderly, at least at Caen and in
Copenhagen, sometimes elect for professional subjects, like
accountancy, but it does not follow that they should become part
of a course intended for those engaged on accountancy as a career.

At Umea in Sweden there exists a project for engaging both
the unemployed and the elderly in data collection for the benefit
of historical demographers, and I think it is fair to say that the
elderly have been much more satisfactory in that role than their
somewhat unwilling companions. It might, of course, turn out
that a high industrial society like our own will finally have to
make the dismal admission that it has got to accept a large body

of unemployed to whom technological re-training is irrelevant, because there never will be jobs enough for them. This would create a situation in which education for leisure or idleness would become a prime demand on the educational system. Even then I would myself retain the view that the elderly would have to be separately handled, in view of the special needs that have already been described.

Limits of traditional adult education

It could be said in general of the history of adult education that it has been a succession of false dawns from the point of view of the educational stimulus of the mass, at least in our country. Neither Extra-mural Boards, nor the WEA, nor the Open University have ever got very far beyond the educational stimulus, of those members of the middle-class, who, for various reasons, have failed to take advantage of higher education at the conventional age, or who, having done so, have felt the need of further instalments later in life. This is true of the Universities of the Third Age in France, nearly two-thirds of whose students come from teaching, commerce and the professions, and it is true of Elderhostel in America, nearly all of whose students are graduates.

However important it is, therefore, to insist that the source of the teaching power for a mass educational programme may well be in the students of our projected third age universities, we must avoid the mistake of supposing that we could so design those institutions that they would themselves reach the mass of the working-class elderly. It has been the failure to appreciate the force of such arguments which has made necessary the introduction of an elementary literacy programme for adults in this country. It is of great significance that these programmes, along with the numeracy programme, pioneered by the National Extention College by the use of television, have had to have recourse to the broadcasting media.

The middle-classes and the mass

As we leave the minor problem for the major problem, the interested and motivated middle-class for the less interested and less motivated mass of the population, three points should perhaps be stressed once more.

The first is the consistent evidence for the stimulus effect which contact or renewed contact gives to elderly persons, and occasionally to their teachers as well. It is this stimulus which the French have in mind when they point to the University of the Third Age as a means by which those in the third age are

prevented as far as and for as long as possible from entering
the fourth age, the age of dependency. Stimulus by education is
enormously cheaper than maintenance, maintenance inside or
outside institutions.

The second point has to do with the understandable disposi-
tion to believe that what works for the motivated, middle-class
elderly, with a youth spent in education and a life spent with the
possibility of re-educating themselves, will work for the much
larger numbers of lower class individuals for whom none of these
things holds true. The third point is a more general one and
plunges us straight into the next section. Further use of air
space for educational purposes must seem unjustifiable if that
educational venture is likely to attract predominantly middle-
class motivated students, of the kind who have in general
responded to the offerings of the Open University. This last
statement implies two things. Firstly, that all further use of
distance teaching by means of broadcasting will have to be so
designed that the mass of the population benefit from it. It
implies, secondly, that since we know as yet so little about the
problem of stimulating the largely unmotivated, a research
programme providing us with the required knowledge is a matter
of the greatest urgency.

(D) Educational stimulus of the uninterested mass
of the elderly population

In Denmark the famous folk high school movement was founded
as long ago as the 1860s to tackle the problem of illiteracy in
the working class. From the very beginning it distanced itself
from the established educational system by disregarding such
traditional educational imperatives as examinations,
qualifications, and the maintenance of universal standards.
The movement had a political origin and its political importance
remains, especially amongst the Danish parties of the left.

Folk high schools exist in Norway too, and all the Scandinavian countries have active pensioners organisations. The
Pensionister Sammwirke of Denmark runs three folk high schools
devoted to the education of the elderly and the other parties also
run such institutions, as do charitable bodies. Organised as they
are, the Danish pensioners have considerable political clout, and
they influence government attitudes towards education for all
elderly people. It is recognized that stimulation of this kind will
help to prevent dependency and institutionalisation. No country
has a more active adult educational movement than Denmark, or
one better financed and organised: no country devotes more
attention to the problems presented by its proportionately

considerable population of elderly people. Yet I was told in
Copenhagen that not one-tenth of the Danish elderly has so far
been reached by educational programmes.

Neither the Norwegians nor the Swedes claim to be more
successful than the Danes in this direction, though the Norwegians made some criticism of the Danes for inefficiency and
extravagance. It seems justifiable to infer from this
Scandinavian evidence that nothing approaching the education
of a majority of elderly people yet exists anywhere, and
certainly not in Britain.

Perhaps it is inappropriate to think of most persons being
involved in education during the third age. Analogies with the
position of younger individuals may be misleading. What is
certain is that no way has yet been found to penetrate the mass
of less educated elderly in any country so as to find out what
their educational needs are. The only instrument which exists
which might make that penetration possible is broadcasting.
It is necessary that we consider its potentialities in some detail.

Use of distance teaching in the educational stimulus
of the mass of the elderly population

Broadcasting is already in use for educational purposes on quite
a large scale in the countries mentioned here. However, such
uses are desultory and unsystematic, except where, as in Britain,
university education along Open University lines has been
instituted. There seems, therefore, to be no experience yet
available for the use of broadcast media for student bodies,
other than those anxious to get degrees, and certainly nothing
about an elderly student body as a subject for educational
stimulus in this way. There are two forms of broadcasting
which can be usefully distinguished: open-ended cultural broadcasting and directed, specifically educational broadcasting.

It is quite evident that cultural programmes have provided
the largest educational stimulus which has reached the mass
viewing and listening audience. This audience in a country like
our own is potentially the whole population, with the elderly
watching and listening even more than the rest. By open ended
is meant literally broadcasting à tous vents - to the four winds -
with no attempt whatever to find out who listens, what the effect
is, 'educational' or otherwise, or to follow up in any way. In
total, the whole number of such broadcasts, all produced for
their intrinsic interest to most people, must in Britain have
enormous impact.

It is also evident that there is in our population a community
of uncertain size on which this impact is scarcely perceptible,

since for them broadcasting is exclusively for diversion. They
never intentionally look at or listen to cultural broadcasting.
Some enlightening or instructional effect exists nevertheless,
even here, if only because of the intellectual content of news
programmes. There is also what used to be called in the BBC
education by stealth, where enlightening items are placed just
after highly popular broadcasts, in the confident knowledge that
a proportion of the audience will fail to switch off when their
favourites have departed. The programme policy of the broadcasting organisations themselves determines how much cultural
broadcasting there shall be and how much education by stealth.
It is very difficult to say what the net effect can be on the elderly,
educationally passive or hostile, typically working-class
British licence holder.

It is clear, therefore, that open ended cultural broadcasting
represents far and away the largest cultural penetration, if that
phrase can be permitted, which takes place in contemporary
society. It is also clear that this deep penetration, represents
the only possible way for the determined educator of the mass of
the elderly to get at his constituency. The obvious way to proceed
is to solicit interested viewers of individual open ended broadcasts, those with some cultural content, to get into touch with
the educational agency, and once this has happened to proceed
with the educational process.

This strategy is now a familiar one, of course, having
already been used by the National Extension College in the
numeracy project, and so on. Any policy proposed for the use
in these directions of the Fourth Channel or any other channel,
must necessarily contain a strategy of this kind. It is in this
way that genuine and potentially fruitful experimentation can be
carried out. But it has to be recognized that in the eyes of most
persons concerned with the educational stimulation of the mass
of the elderly at the present time, broadcasting of whatever kind,
open-ended or otherwise, and particularly television, is regarded
in a very equivocal fashion.

The Dangers of television
Many discussing the possible use of these methods insist on the
fact that the tendency of the old to be passive, to diminish their
contacts with those outside the home, to lose sources of stimulus
which were always present when they had to go daily out to work,
and to care for their children - a process described by gerontologists as that of disengagement - was intensified by watching
television. Indeed in the opinion of some, television was the
typical instrument used by those who relapsed into isolation and

withdrawal. A Norwegian expert, Mrs Beverfeldt in Oslo, for example, judged television to be the enemy of the elderly.

In her view it keeps them within the household and impoverishes their social relations, interrupting their conversation with those who visit them, who have to compete with the moving screen. In her view it even interferes with their relationships with their children and others of great importance to them. As a substitute for these human relationships, however, television viewing addicts the elderly to a nullity, since the image cannot itself offer human companionship, or anything at all in the way of emotional sustenance. Television dependence, she felt, was unlikely to be of use in furthering the educational stimulus of the aged for all these reasons, the most important being that it was the usual explanation given why elderly individuals failed to take part in those social occasions, which it is one of the great merits of an educational programme to make necessary. I was told in Oslo that older people will not attend Norwegian folk high schools at such times as high audience television programmes are being broadcast, and this must be a very widespread experience.

Here we reach the crux of the use of broadcasting for the educational stimulus of the mass of the elderly, and it is beyond my information and experience to take the discussion further. The position seems to me to be as follows. Broadcasting, including sound broadcasting, is by far the most important experiential fact in their lives from the point of view of education, and yet it has these undesirable effects from the educational point of view. Television dependency is something which may perhaps diminish over time, and ways may perhaps be found to lessen its extent and its intensity. There is no reason to believe that much can be accomplished in these directions. We must simply become accustomed to the use of an instrument which has this two-edged quality. What is wanted is hard information and a policy.

Directed broadcasting and the educational stimulus of the elderly

Broadcasting specifically directed towards the elderly need not be confined to educational purposes. Programmes consisting almost entirely of diversion particularly acceptable to the elderly have been regularly transmitted in Scandinavia: items of useful information for this audience are mixed in with the amusement. It has to be said that some of the officials concerned with the welfare of the old who have described these programmes to me, found them intolerable to watch or to listen to. So trivial and superficial were most of their contents that they were unacceptable to the highly educated, serious minded, relatively youthful, middle-class person.

I take this to be a fact of some significance for the following reasons. It could well turn out that there would be considerable criticism and even some active opposition from well-intentioned interested parties to the broadcasting of educational material discovered through research to be well suited to the educational stimulus of the mass working-class elderly. Those who arranged the numeracy and literacy programmes may already have experienced something of this kind. The fact seems to be that the material which may have to be presented will lack all of the 'elevating' associations which attach to the open-ended cultural broadcasting items we have been discussing. It will be bound to seem trivial to those who find it difficult to imagine not being possessed of the type of information which has to be concentrated upon and for whom the pace and manner of delivery is tedious. What is true for broadcasting, of course, would be true for the whole content of a mass educational undertaking.

Some research suggests that the elderly, even the highly educated elderly, slow down as learners, that they are not as quick to make inferences and are more easily confused, that their rate of processing is slower and that they have more trouble with the spoken word as against the written word. Repetition and pauses are necessary. Given these, however, their comprehensional ability to absorb is not in question. A point of interest is that they have formidable difficulties with negative information, which is daunting at all ages. It is also true that much more has to be learnt about such subjects.

Now that the possible difficulties and the obvious drawbacks of the use of television and radio for the distance teaching of the elderly have been explored, it might be useful to list its advantages.

i. Broadcasting is the only means of access to virtually every single person, whether at home or in an institution. This is the major reason why almost everyone at all engaged with the educational stimulus of the elderly readily agrees that access to broadcasting would be an enormous advantage, in spite of the dangers of television.

ii. Broadcasting is decidedly the most flexible of all methods of educational communication. Because of recent and coming developments, it is no longer confined to spoken word programmes in that print can now be transmitted. The development of video tape cassettes will mean that visual items can be played over to himself, when he wishes, by the pupil, just as is now usual in

distance teaching in the Open University in the case of sound
cassettes.

iii. Broadcasting is the only method of instruction which does
not require travel, peculiarly important to a student body less
likely to have access to cars and more likely not to be in a
position to drive them. The general importance of this for a
mass programme should not be overlooked. If we ⸱succeeded
in assembling really large masses of the population at particular
points for educational purposes, we should create a massive
traffic problem too. There is also the consideration of the use
of fuel and other resources.

iv. Broadcasting is now an established, customary channel of
communication for all public purposes, and is so regarded by
its audiences.

v. Broadcast teaching can and should always be of the highest
technical standard using a fund of illustrative and expository
materials not available to the small class teacher, the lessons
being conducted according to the best known methods. Such
lessons can be rehearsed before recording, perfected in every
possible way, and repeated at will, over the air and otherwise.

vi. Broadcasting can reach the illiterate, even the near-sighted,
the deaf, the house-bound, the bedridden.

vii. If properly organised and handled, broadcasting should
simply be cheaper than all other forms of teaching, and if pursued
on a truly mass scale, it could be very cheap indeed.

viii. Broadcasting is so universal a characteristic of present
communications from the outside world to the individual, that
it could even be said that he has a right to receive educational
stimulation from it. On this consideration, he should not be
required to make the effort of leaving his own surroundings to
visit a distant gathering point simply for the purpose of
absorbing information.

ix. In Britain we have a tradition of excellence in broadcasting,
which gives it a standing in the community, a reputation with the
intellectuals and a general authority quite unparallelled in any
other country which I know. This is true of the commercial
television and radio companies as well as of the BBC itself.
Since the foundation of the Open University, moreover, we have
developed a unique tradition of distance teaching using this medium.

x. In spite of its universality, television still fascinates viewers
and everything televised is still thought of as to some degree
special. This fact might help to compensate for the loss of all
association with high social status which may characterise the
educational stimulus of the mass of the elderly.

xi. In Britain, under present circumstances, with our resources for such an undertaking as stimulating the mass elderly by educational means being so very limited, with no prospect of a professional teaching body being established for the purpose and with the cost of travel to and from classes increasing as it is, distance teaching may be the only expedient open to us. If the ageing of the population had occurred before the development of distance teaching on television and sound radio, our dilemma would have been even greater.

Having listed the advantages and opportunities presented by the use of directed broadcasting for the purpose we have in mind, we must face its limitations and disadvantages as well. Apart from those which it shares with open-ended broadcasting, there is the fact that information delivered by broadcast means is apparently not very easily retained. Teaching, moreover, cannot be confined to the delivery of an address, however well constructed and effective. Response from the student is indispensible and in the case of distance teaching, this must imply writing letters, if not exercises. Letter writing does not come at all easily even to the literate amongst the badly educated, the elderly especially.

These considerations may negate some of the listed advantages of directed broadcasting in distance teaching to the elderly or at least seriously diminish their importance. It is notable that the Open University has found television of much less significance as a direct teaching instrument than was expected by those who pioneered it, and it is said that the Open University could do without its reserved television time. Its teaching, as is well known, has come to consist much more in correspondence lessons using the remarkable course books which have been developed, than in visual or sound broadcasts, though sound cassettes are apparently of considerable value to students.

But correspondence teaching, it is clear, makes just the type of demand on the elderly student which the working-class man and woman find unwelcome and are indeed often unable to cope with. It has been found, moreover, that reading by oneself, regarded at present as essential for education by any method, but peculiarly important in the case of distance teaching, is precisely that which those with insufficient schooling in early life are least likely to want to do. An important reason for their being in need of intellectual stimulus is because they do not habitually read, and one of the reasons why television plays such an important part in their leisure is because it occupies them without requiring the effort of reading. There has to be added to this the point that the near-sighted and hard of hearing are able to respond much less readily to broadcasting than others and that the illiterate would be in no position to follow written instructions on the screen.

If the limitations of directed broadcasting are pursued up to this point and beyond, however, they soon become identical with the general difficulties of attempting educational stimulus of the passive mass of the elderly population. They reveal once again how little tested and accurate knowledge we have of such things and how great is the urgency of a properly established research effort to repair our ignorance. Before we turn to this, further comment should perhaps be made about the educational stimulus of the working-class mass of the population.

High intelligence, personal effectiveness, a mastery of the art of living, are associated with long years of educational experience at all ages and all levels in a society. But the two are never identical, and it is quite remarkable how impressive are the abilities, imaginative and intellectual as well as practical capacities, of working-class persons lacking formal education later than the age of twelve or thirteen. They have a quality which it is very hard to define. The most difficult problem facing the designer of a method of providing educational stimulus for the mass of the working-class elderly is to find a way both of respecting and making use of this peculiarly elusive characteristic of such persons.

(E) Topics on which new knowledge is essential if a
      practicable programme is to be designed

This final section begins with a discussion of the present position of relevant research in Britain and continues with a list of the topics which should be pursued. No plan of a research policy is offered as such, since it should arise in the course of experimentation with the use of television in the stimulation of the mass of the elderly.

Gerontology has grown up, as might be expected, around the medical profession and most of the scientific information about the aged and the process of ageing is physiological. Gerontological medicine is a fast growing specialism, which is to be expected since an increasing proportion of hospital beds is now filled with elderly people. The medical profession and the hospital system in fact is almost wholly responsible for the care and even for the maintenance of those who have reached the fourth age and for their experience when dying. Preparation for death could well be called the most demanding of all educational duties. The responsibilities of doctors and nurses in these directions are bound to grow with the rapid expansion of the highest age groups.

Under these circumstances it is understandable that there is a very urgent need for knowledge on how it might be possible to make the elderly less dependent, more active, less likely to enter the fourth age. Hospitals for the elderly are already committed to keeping their patients within the community for as long as possible and are ceasing to accept cases for which there is any hope whatever of some sort of active life being pursued outside the institution. If it is true that the educational stimulus of the mass of the elderly could do even a small amount to prevent or postpone the attainment of the fourth age, quite apart from the assistance it might be to marginal persons still kept within the community, then it would be a relief to the medical services and a saving of resources, social as well as financial. Any new knowledge on the issues we have been discussing, therefore, must be regarded as crucial, and valuable from the point of view of efficiency.

Doctors are most decidedly not the only persons concerned with the aged, for the welfare services generally, voluntary and public, are more and more seriously engaged with them. Care of the old has been a traditional object of charity and of voluntary public service. Those who provide, or give their voluntary assistance to, day centres, homes for the elderly, housing for the elderly, meals on wheels, visits to the elderly and so on, are all likewise deeply interested in keeping the elderly as active, interested and socially involved as possible. They want them to be able to live their lives independently and away from expensive institutions, just as those who run those institutions want to know how to keep their inmates as active and alert as possible. Any knowledge, once again, any knowledge, of how to provide educational stimulus for the elderly would be of interest to a very wide circle indeed. It could only lead to an economy of resources.

Perhaps I may be allowed to pause at this point and illustrate the issue by two personal experiences. In 1948 I had occasion to visit for the BBC one of the most distinguished scientists then alive, Sir Charles Sherrington, aged 92 in that year. He was a former President of the Royal Society, which had recently held a meeting in his bedroom in the nursing home where he was living. When I presented myself there, I was informed by the sister-in-charge that, although Sir Charles was bedridden and infirm, he was a very intelligent man and was not to be spoken to as a child. Evidently in this particular case, no way had been found to keep such a man in continued and continual contact with his intellectual interests.

The Education of the Elderly in Britain

In the model day care centre belonging to the city of Copenhagen, in September 1979, I was shown the books on the shelves of the library. Many of them were large improving works, little borrowed and not of much use for the majority of the elderly who visited the place. Most used, of course, was the fiction and what everybody would call light literature, but nothing approaching the pornographic was to be seen. Even in the city of Copenhagen, the elderly were apparently being prevented from taking part in a literary and aesthetic movement of great vigour and importance at that time.

It is difficult to say how far occurrences of this kind are due to mistakes and inefficiency and how far to ignorance about what the elderly would want and what they would respond to. Nevertheless it is easy to fall into what might be called the pathetic fallacy of the educational idealist in respect of the aged, which brings us to our educational dilemma.

In an article published in 1978 brief reference was made to the fifth educational right set out above, the right to respect the elderly in recognition of their unique intellectual and cultural value. The same illustration, the pursuit of classical languages, was used and I found myself discussing the proposition with an old lady, once a school teacher, 86 years old and going blind. She was doubly offended, and felt rebuffed. 'Do you really expect me to take up Latin and Greek at my age? Am I to feel inadequate if I have no wish whatever to exert myself intellectually? Have I not earned the right to spend my time as I wish and to avoid any exertion which is not attractive to me?'

There are echoes here of the socially compulsive character of the traditional educational system, of the shaming expedients so widely used by would-be improvers of the mind. But once more the predominant impression is about our ignorance: we simply do not know enough about the attitudes, tastes, desires, capacities, of those whom we wish to influence for their good, as we believe, and for the good of the society which we share.

The following list refers for the most part to subjects already touched upon as important to the educational stimulus of the elderly and yet subjects on which little and sometimes nothing is so far known. Some of the topics require investigation at the fundamental level and presumably would have to be tackled by psychological laboratories and university departments of education. This is in addition to such subjects as the relative learning capacity of the elderly on which work is in train. Most of the points listed, however, could be illuminated by small scale experimentation, making greater or lesser use of broadcasting, especially television. The topics are -

i.   to discover all that is possible about the relationship of intellectual stimulation and the process of social ageing, disengagement and the growth of dependency.

ii.   to determine the attitude of elderly persons towards education, educational institutions and the traditional curricula. To discover how far association with official, middle-class institutions and authoritarian treatment at school may be responsible for indifference or hostility.

iii.   to establish what most interests the elderly person in relation to his own educational level, and his (her) experience since leaving school. To find ways of satisfying that interest in matters of presentation, teaching method, and to relate all these with years of schooling, subsequent job experience, income, reading and writing skills and so on.

iv.   to investigate what motivation there can be to learn when what is learnt can have no effect on subsequent life chances, where emulation is largely absent, and when useful learning can only be a small category.

v.   to evaluate possible methods of follow-up after an initial broadcasting break-through. The methods used must be calculated to be effective with those whose reading and writing skills are modest, who may find class participation difficult and who may for the most part be unwilling to do anything on their own between teaching occasions.

vi.   to give a great deal of attention to the mix between broadcasting, correspondence, class attendance and private study, in relation to the elderly student body and to develop a recipe or series   of   recipes suited to varying levels of previous experience, contact with education and so on. In doing this, to balance the importance of elderly pupils meeting each other out of the house against their right to be taught at home and the trouble and expense of travel. Included in such experiments would be bedridden elderly and those in institutions.

vii.   to locate retired people able and willing to become active in stimulating the mass of the elderly educationally. To make use of existing institutions initially, but to continue with members of Universities of the Third Age.

viii.   to study exhaustively the intellectual situation of those with failing hearing and failing sight. To consider the position of those in homes and hospitals in relation to nursing and administrative staff.

ix.   to investigate the difficulties associated with television as an educational medium and to discover ways, if such exist, to compensate against television dependence.

x.   to research into the attitudes and personal history of those who respond favourably to experimentation of this kind, and, which is perhaps more important, to do the same for those who fail to respond or who drop out.

xi. to survey the potentialities for the educational stimulus of the elderly of the whole range of institutions and established activities which might be of value. Apart from universities, schools, colleges, broadcasting organisations and so on, considered in this report, there is a series of others not mentioned. They include the following -

The network of public libraries.

Local societies with intellectual pursuits, especially archaeological and historical societies, literary circles, those devoted to painting and so on, and including folk dance societies, singing clubs, etc.

The National Trust, which manages so many houses and sites particularly well suited to teaching visits: the Department of the Environment in the same context.

xii. to investigate all possible organisational forms and methods of development of a programme for the purposes in hand, bearing in mind the enormous numbers of a possible student body and the obvious dangers of gigantism and administrative overload. To consider carefully the trade union rights of teachers in employment and in retirement in relation to a teaching body for the educational stimulus of the elderly. To discover ways of building up a structure from small beginnings and in the localities. A loose federation would, it is hoped, be brought into being rather than a nationwide organisation of a bureaucratic kind.

It is not difficult to justify the judgment that the measure of the extent to which a society can be called civilised can be found in its older people and their treatment. Nor is it possible for the educator to deny that the supreme test of its activity is how he would approach persons whose only reason for learning is enlightenment, intellectual and aesthetic satisfaction. Everyone of us is challenged by the education of the elderly and challenged in a way in which we can all do something about.

Chapter 3

CONTEMPLATING THE DEVELOPMENT OF
UNIVERSITIES OF THE THIRD AGE

MICHEL PHILIBERT

With a grasp of English somewhat shaming to we natives,
Michel Philibert does much more than recall the French
origins of the Université du Troisième Age. He reflects on
the functions of this new institution, underlining the benefits
of socialisation, the opportunities to structure our unprecedented free-time, the chance to provide 'a yeast of regener-
ation for the entire academic community', and the scope
available for the autonomous design of one's own learning.
In a brilliant flourish, he concludes with an impressively
persuasive appeal to sustain learning into the ripest old age
and to reinterpret such learning constantly for the profit of
all mankind. It is strongly apparent how the English counterparts of the French U3As have embraced the spirit, if not
always the letter, of continental practice, especially with
regard to the right of members to determine their own
patterns of learning, the social value of lifelong educational
provision, and the U3A critique-in-practice of the
conventional educational mode.
Professeur Michel Philibert, a celebrated scholar of the
University of Grenoble, has been associated with the continental U3A movement in Grenoble and elsewhere since its
origins twelve years ago.

Pierre Vellas, University Professor of Political Economy,
baptized L'Université du Troisième Age with a programme of
lectures, concerts, guided tours and other cultural activities,
which he offered in 1972, as a summer school to retired persons
in Toulouse: he planned to accommodate in the halls and classrooms of the local University, deserted at this time of year,
those older people who would respond.
    Like all actors in human history, and the more so all pioneers
and innovators, Vellas 'did not know what he was doing'. When

51

after a few weeks, the programme came to an end, such were
the enthusiasm and determination of the participants, that,
instead of preparing a repeat for the next summer, Vellas was
forced to launch a programme for the forth-coming academic
year, to find rooms, lectures and tutors, very soon to arrange
satellite programmes in cities around Toulouse, and to comment
on this experience on radio and television. In no time similar
undertakings mushroomed in France and abroad, a first
international colloquium on the new concept was held in Toulouse
as early as May 1973, and an international Federation of Third
Age Universities established.

Now, after ten years of development, can one tell the kind
of future to which Third Age Universities are heading? Their
development reveals a diversity of structures and a multiplicity
of functions that makes any prognosis most uncertain. We shall
not venture a prediction. We shall limit the ambition of this
short essay to sketch out two contrasted hypotheses: their use,
at the cost of oversimplifying, might eventually help us to
decipher, interpret, and possibly influence, further developments.

Oversimplifying, then, we wonder whether the Universities
of the Third Age will prove to have been the rear-guard or the
avant-garde of a historical evolution of 'standard' universities,
aiming to both adapt themselves to, and be rejuvenated by, new
partners and new problems. In other terms, will these recently
developing institutions, the Grand-Ma's University, appear in the
coming decades as having been a futile and vain attempt to re-
enact Daddy's University, or as an inspired, urgently needed,
and successful effort, to repattern the whole fabric of our
educational set-up, and, borrowing Ivan Illitch's phrase, to
deschool our society?

(A) The Functions of Universities of the Third Age
Among other possible functions of Third Age Universities we
shall mention the following, after two preliminary remarks:
First, any organisation or institution may have several simultaneous or successive functions; and, second, most human
undertakings are meant to achieve some end, or willed effect,
but have side-effects that may go beyond or against the agent's
will, unplanned, unforeseen, and for some time unperceived by
him and his contemporaries. So the functions of U3As we are
going to describe are neither mutually incompatible nor exhaust
the analysis. Their mention and evaluation is meant as a tool to
accentuate or minimize some of these functions and thereby
repattern the institutions.
i. U3As contribute to help socialise or to re-socialize

retired people. Both increasing longevity and decreasing birth-
rates make for a percentage of older persons greater than in
earlier times without any family left, while generalised retirement either weakens or destroys lifelong networks of relationships with partners, colleagues, employees and clients.
Isolation, and possibly loneliness, threaten retired and older
persons. U3As provide a minority of them with a space for
meeting and interaction not only with 'age-peers', but with three
generations of people from fifty to some ninety years old, and
often with opportunities for organized interaction with groups
and individuals of various ages.

Other associations, clubs and communities, some open only
to retired persons, senior citizens and veterans, some recruit-
ing without age-discrimination, offer similar opportunities.
But the very development of U3As, as well as the first surveys
available, suggest the reality of this function of re-socialization.
ii. U3As provide opportunities, stimulation, patterns and content
for the use and structure of the free-time that our society gives
to (or inflicts upon) those who, willy-nilly, and sometimes
suddenly, disengage from paid work, from habits and schedules
in-grown over decades. Assignments and social expectations
that might have appeared, and be resented, as constraints
reveal, when they disappear, that they were playing in our lives
a structuring, supporting, cohesive role. U3As allow their
members to use and structure their time in the pursuit of
knowledge: it may be for knowledge's sake, for the pleasure of
learning and understanding, or of developing new mental skills,
for personal growth and fulfilment; it may be for preparing
themselves for new roles, pursuits and activities, for making
themselves more pleasant or more useful for family, friends,
peers or the community, through mutual help and voluntary
service. Let us not altogether forget satisfactions found in
self-esteem or vanity, the challenge of competition, the
pleasure in being praised or admired for one's progresses
and achievements.

However powerful and ambiguous the individual motivations
for studying may be, the older learner is not likely, as most
young students and quite a few among younger adult learners, to
be prompted to study mainly in order to get a position or a
promotion, to become a more efficient and better paid producer,
to make money, neither (with qualifications) to increase his
power. Inasmuch as this is correct, a new function of U3As
emerges, not just for their individual members but for the
learning and teaching community at large, for the network of
educational institutions, and their own function in the community.

iii. To the extent they contribute to promote, or to restore, knowledge for the sake of knowledge, U 3As underline a dimension of knowledge that contemporary society, and not only its individual members, tends to obfuscate or indeed to pervert. We perceive knowledge as a tool for progress in efficiency, for increase in production and in productivity, for earning a living or making a fortune, for developing our power, whether personal, tribal or national, not only over our environment, but over people: other individuals, groups, nations, so as to control, abuse and exploit them. Knowledge indeed provides us with such tools. But leaving aside, for one moment, the moral and political situation in which mankind now finds itself - a most dangerous and explosive one - the status of knowledge itself might prove more precarious than its recent and dramatic progress and efficiency lead us to believe.

For centuries, science has very slowly and progressively disengaged from current opinions and beliefs, from ancient myths, from theology and ideology - in constant and dialectical interaction with philosophy - and it has been practiced and elaborated by amateurs. At first view, the accelerated pace of its progress through the 19th and more so in the 20th centuries may be explained by the fact that, beginning with the French Revolution, Western nations, once convinced science could pay in power and efficiency, made scientists paid workers and exponentially multiplied public money invested in scientific research and teaching. But that is only one side of the coin. Inasmuch as science progresses through reiteration, duplication and generalisation of what is already known, the more scientists you pay, the more rapid the pace of progress, the greater the bulk of knowledge. Once penicillin was found, due to Fleming and mainly to René Dubos, hundreds of scientists found out aureomycine, streptomycine, and many others along the same pattern.

But science progresses also by correction of former notions, revision of concepts, changes of paradigms, by borrowing from one field a concept, a method, an instrument or an hypothesis, and transplanting it in a different field, by repatterning vast areas of knowledge and expelling out of its temple previously held theories and worn-out methodologies. To that extent these progresses seem to have been made in the last two centuries by a relatively small number of individuals - and to have been grounded, in mathematics and in the experimental sciences of nature (astronomy, physics, chemistry, biology) on a basis of philosophical and scientific principles laid out by the great amateur scientist over more than two thousand years. The

confusion that presides over the so-called moral, or social, or
human sciences, mostly the competing sociologies and psycholo-
gies and political economies (with the possible exception of
anthropology, history and linguistics) demonstrates in our view
the incapacity of the professional paid scientists, victimized by
hyperspecialization, tribalism, and current or 'scientific'
ideologies, to progress significantly on a ground that has not
been prepared and fertilised by centuries of amateur science.
And the hypothesis that even in the hard sciences the rates of
productivity of research (not in quantity of publications, but in
scientific quality) might now be decreasing, seems plausible.

To that extent, the gratuitous, amateurish character of U3A
learning, study and research might become a yeast of regenera-
tion for the entire academic community. The same could obtain,
as we shall submit in the next paragraph, as regards the U3A
teaching procedures.

iv. The French school system leaves to the children, as pupils,
and French Universities to young people, as students, practically
no autonomy in the design, the pace, the schedule and the content
of their study; their learning is parcelled out into small bits and
pieces. Teachers lead them not so much on the ground of the
authority that their knowledge, and their ability to share it,
could support, but because as grown-ups, they are more or less
in loco parentis, and as civil servants, representatives of the
ruling political and social system. One should expect that, in
continued education, in adult education, learners would be more
critical of mediocre teachers, more autonomous in designing
and managing their own learning; one might hope that the
redevelopment (in France) of adult education, would teach the
teachers new ways of teaching, more respectful of the initiative,
interest and idiosyncrasies of their students; one might hope
these teachers (and their students as parents) would transfer to
schools these new and better methods, for the benefit of children.
But it did not, it does not currently happen, for two reasons:
firstly, after fifteen to twenty-five years of schooling, most
adults are either so disgusted by education that they will never
venture into continued education, or so well adjusted to the
system that they will never imagine that learning might be anything else than being fed with ready-made thoughts by teachers
who know better. Secondly, the most frequent motivation (in
France) for venturing into continued education is to get a
diploma and a better salary or position, and the best way to
achieve this is to learn uncritically whatever the teacher teaches,
so as to pass the examination in repeating him verbatim what
he said.

To be frank, some of the older and retired learners, members of U3As, have the same receptive and sometimes passive, approach as their juniors; with U3A audiences often more respectful of Universities and Professors than younger students. This is an effect of generation, not of age, and they have to bear with quite a few lecturers who, finding them more polite and more grateful than rebellious children or angry, anxious and bitter students, indulge in conceit, pomposity, tyranny and revenge.

Despite such adverse circumstances, U3A audiences include a higher percentage than the average population of liberated, bold and creative men and women, who do not attend because they are after money, power, position or prestige, and are quite able to teach their teachers better ways.

v. The last function of U3As that we shall mention here is that their 'third age' participants, inasmuch as they demand to be treated as partners, and not merely as objects of research, as participants in study, and not merely as receptacles of teaching, may well use the opportunity to prepare themselves for a new period of their life, for new tasks and commitments. We have indeed mentioned this point in our paragraph - 'preparing themselves for new roles, pursuits, and activities' - but we want to add that 'old age' today is not only a new period (and the last) in the life course of the individual. It is today a new period in the history of mankind. This will be elaborated on in the last part of this chapter.

And yet U3As are threatened by elitism and by age-segregation. The trouble here is perhaps less age-segregation per se than its use as a decoy to camouflage, under the ambiguous label 'third age', a middle-class, elitist discrimination against lower-middle and working classes.

U3As are exposed to the risk of being used as an innocent, enjoyable, and finally futile pastime. Let us remember what Montaigne wrote in the last chapter of his _Essays_; he is very near the end of the book and not so far from the end of his life: 'I have a vocabulary all my own. I pass the time, when it is rainy and disagreable; when it is good, I do not want to pass it; I savor it, I cling to it. We must run through the bad and settle on the good. This ordinary expression "pastime" or "pass the time" represents the habit of those wise folk who think they can make no better use of their life than to let it slip by and escape it, pass it by, sidestep it, and, as far as in them lies, ignore it and run away from it, as something irksome and contemptible. But I know it to be otherwise and find it both agreeable and worth prizing, even in its last decline, in which I now possess it; and

nature has placed it in our hands adorned with such favourable
conditions that we have only ourselves to blame if it weighs on us
and if it escapes us unprofitably. "The life of the fool is joyless,
full of trepidation, given over wholly to the future (Seneca)".
However, I am reconciling myself to the thought of losing it
without regret, but as something that by its nature must be lost;
not as something annoying and troublesome. Then too, not to
dislike dying is properly becoming only to those who like living.
It takes management to enjoy life. I enjoy it twice as much as
others, for the measure of enjoyment depends on the greater or
lesser attention that we lend it. Especially at this moment, when
I perceive that mine is so brief in time, I try to increase it in
weight; I try to arrest the speed of its flight by the speed with
which I grasp it, and to compensate for the haste of its ebb by my
vigor in using it. The shorter my possession of life, the deeper
and fuller I must make it'. (Montaigne, Essays, transl. Donald
M. Frame, Stanford Univ. Press (1957) p. 853).

Threatened - or tempted - by elitism and pastime activism,
U3As might indulge in narcissism and escapism and miss
altogether the highest vocation they should respond to. Before
briefly formulating how we conceive it, let us analyze the
perennial and continuing motivations that make continued
education a must for each and every human being, and demand
from older people the highest achievements.

(B) Universities of the Third Age: Discerning the Signs of the Times.
Frank Harris in My Life and Loves gives praise to Alfred Russell
Wallace's 'very simple and great nature' in the following terms:
'It is by the heart we grow, and Wallace kept himself so sincere,
so kindly, that he grew in wisdom to the very end of his life
instead of stopping, as most men and women stop growing mentally
almost before their bodily growth is completed'.

The new born human baby is in a condition of incapacity,
ignorance, and dependency from his elders and betters more
radical than the offspring of any other animal species. He is
also endowed with a need, a desire, and a capacity to learn, to
acquire knowledge and know-hows, far exceeding that of other
animals. Children will learn more, more easily and more
rapidly, through the first years of their lives, than later on.
But there is so much to learn to be able to function autonomously
that a number of years is necessary, sometimes less than the
number required to reach their full size and complete their bodily
growth. But about that time, they will usually master roughly the
equivalent in knowledge and skills of most grown ups; they will be
accepted as such and will become in their turn workers, producers,

soldiers, parents, caregivers, educators, citizens. Throughout childhood and early youth, their main occupation is learning. Once engaged in work, parenthood, trade, responsibilities, some people do, and some do not, keep on learning. In many cases, as remarks Harris, 'people stop growing mentally', they stop learning, using till they die the stock of knowledge and capacities they have acquired in their first and only years of learning. Humans can stop learning, but they ought not.

So great are the ignorance and dependency of infants and young children that they have to receive from parents or elders most of the knowledge and skills, including mental skills, to speak, to listen, to think, to discipline emotions and feelings, attitudes and behaviour. Among the three classical definitions of truth - agreement with other minds, agreement with reality, agreement of the mind with itself through its successive statements - the child cannot but begin by agreeing with others. Thus the child, while acquiring indispensable mental skills, notions, ways, and many useful bits and pieces of knowledge, theoretical and pragmatic, will also receive, accept and make his own, a huge amount of myths, stereotypes, prejudices, biases, errors, delusions and nonsense, and inevitably will harbour them as being right, true, normal, obvious and congenial. Error having the same form and the same function as the truth, he will not search for a truth he believes he already possesses; he may well reject, deny and fight the truth, if and when it will cross his mind, as being antagonistic with what he takes for true.

This explains why he can, and should, keep on learning. The most difficult and important part of learning begins when the first stock, needed for practical purposes, is acquired; and it consists mostly in un-learning, in de-learning, what one has been learning so far. It is a task to be pursued over the entire life course, and we shall die, even in advanced old age, without having done with it.

Mankind has known for a long time that growing old does not entail growing wiser. 'It is not only the old who are wise, or the aged who understand what is right', says young Elihu in the Book of Job, angry with the three older friends of Job, unable to persuade him of his guilt. His Fool says to Lear: 'If thou wert my fool, n'uncle, I'd have thee beaten for being old before thy time'. Lear: 'How's that?' Fool: 'Thou should'st not have been old till thou hadst been wise'.

But if age is not a sufficient condition to reach wisdom, and, if a few young people exhibit a maturity far exceeding their years, age usually remains a necessary condition to advance in wisdom, because truth can appear only as correction of a former error;

wisdom grows when we begin to understand in retrospect that we did not know what we were doing, we did not will what we figured we wanted, we did not experience what we fancied feeling.

Any action, experience, event or sequence in our past lives we have been interpreting already at least three times. We gave it a first meaning in anticipation: project and prevision, fear, hope and expectation, prayer, wish, preparation and prevention, reasoning and fancying. Then it occurred; we acted, or suffered, we were in medias res; and it was more or less different from our anticipation; we had to readjust our behaviour, to modify our strategy, to reappraise our ends and means, our capacities and our shortcomings, to reinterpret the situation, to repattern our projects. Later on, when we look in retrospect at the past event, we do not give it the meaning we gave it in anticipation, neither the meaning it suggested when present. It has been developing unwilled effects, unanticipated consequences, it now appears in a different context, filled up by all that we went through since it happened; and our criteria to rate its importance, to assess its meaning, may have changed over time: they are our present tastes and convictions, engagements and responsibilities, our present projects and expectations, fears and hopes. If we do not stop growing, we shall have to reinterpret our life till the end; its unity and meaning must be recreated every day, we must reinterpret and redirect it in integrating what our own deeds and words, our own whims and fancies, and the accidents and the necessities have brought into it.

The most important task of older people is the reinter- pretation of their life. It is important to them. It is no less important to all of us, because their lives have been shared and mixed with those of their parents, siblings, mates, partners, children, colleagues, fellow workers and citizens, with the history of their village and nation, of their profession and creed, with a sequence in Man's History; and we need whatever light their reinterpretation, their evaluation, their repentance may shed on our own life and history, so as to know how we wish and should orientate and lead it from where we are now. Here lies the most important task and function that U3A should systema- tically develop.

This reinterpretation of their own life and our common history has always been the most outstanding contribution of older people to their community and to the human community.

It is today more important than ever before. Not only it is the first time in human history that most people born alive have a chance to live into old age; not only it is the first time in human history that we have so many older people available to help us confronting our experiences and expectations, reinterpreting our experiences and redirecting our expectations; not only it is the first time in human history that people from three to five different generations can coexist and interact for so many years and decades, and this potential has not been really explored and exploited, but it is also the first time in human history that mankind is challenged to find out the ways to live as one - because for the first time in its history it has conquered the actual capacity to destroy itself as one, once and for all. Like King Lear, many old fools could age and die, in their last decades, before having been wise. But never before our days have human fools been given the capacity of destroying the human kind. Our foolishness is more dangerous than it ever was, because never before has the gap been so wide between our science and power, and our continued lack of wisdom; never before has the human need of wisdom been so urgent. The two or three generations of older people now living are and will remain unique in the history of mankind. They are the last living humans born in the prenuclear period of history. They are the last and the first older people in history whose search and strife for wisdom must succeed, if history is to continue.

Some sixty years ago George Stanley Hall - a prophetic soul! - wrote in his book <u>Senescence</u>: 'There is a rapport between us oldsters and we understand each other almost esoterically. We must accept and recognize this better knowledge of this stage of life as part of our present duty in the community......... We have a function in the world that we have not yet risen to and which is of the utmost importance - far greater, in fact, in the present stage of the world than ever before, and that new and culminating service can only be seen and prepared for by first realizing what ripe and normal age is, means, can, should and now must do, if our race is to achieve its true goal'.

Do these words convey the dreams of an old fool, or the lucid deciphering of our time by a wise old man? Reader, decide.

Chapter 4

THE INTERNATIONAL PERSPECTIVE FOR U3As

DAVID RADCLIFFE

David Radcliffe, associate professor of the Faculty of
Education, University of Western Ontario, is a comparative
educationist with a specialist reputation in educational
gerontology. In 1980-81 he spent a year's study leave with
Age Concern England and the Extra-Mural Studies Department of the University of London during which he surveyed
recent developments in educational opportunities for the
elderly in Western Europe. It would be difficult to find
anyone better to place the first stirrings of British activity
in a worldwide context.

In several instances in this chapter he quotes his own
translations from other languages, avoiding over-literal
awkwardnesses and helpfully using English idioms which
carry the proper sense of the original.

(A) Fire from Olympus
Philippe Aries in his book L'enfance et la vie familiale sous
l'ancien régime (Paris 1960), published in England as Centuries
of Childhood (London 1962), drew attention to the 'discovery' of
childhood in the sixteenth and seventeenth centuries. He related
this to the development of formal schooling, and to the dominant
model for education systems and learning opportunities which
are primarily linked to childhood and adolescence. The concept
of adolescence emerged in the late nineteenth century, and some
would argue that adolescence has been the preferred age of the
mid-twentieth century. But we are perhaps on the brink of an
even more dramatic change in the perception of the human life-
course with the emergence, in the late twentieth century, of what
the French have chosen to call the Third Age, 'Le Troisième
Age'. As defined by Serge Mayence, second president of the
International Association of Universities of the Third Age, ' The
third age is that time of life when, having ceased any occupational

activity, men and women enjoy total independence.' In other
words, it corresponds to retirement from 'the world of work',
but it includes an assertion that this is a whole new age, with
its own validity to be established. It can be distinguished from
'le quatrième âge', the fourth age of renewed and increasing
dependence on others, but the two are closely related, for third
age thought being implicitly positive, carries the belief that with
appropriate recognition, acceptance, and emphasis, a good third
age can minimize the adjustments and deficits, and indeed the
duration of the fourth age.

There is a great deal of demographic justification in the
sociological perception of the Third Age as a whole new age in
human experience, without historical precedent, for although it
seems that three-score years and ten (or by latest calculations
four-score years and five) has always been mankind's optimum
lot, never before has such a large proportion of the population
had reasonable expectations of attaining it. We are therefore
dealing with a 'whole new age for the old', as Maggie Kuhn,
founder of the American Gray Panthers, has put it. But, in
examining the popular movement that has led to the establishment
of the Universities of the Third Age in France, and which has
rapidly attracted international attention and spread to other
countries, it is important at the outset to recognise another
element, another axis which cuts across the ageing dimension.
This is the dimension of social status and occupation; employment
and participation; social worth and self respect. While the
Universities of the Third Age have developed in response to needs
that are particularly perceived by older persons who have retired
from the years of occupational activity and status, and who seek
to turn this erstwhile retreat into an advance into a new autonomy
of life-style, these needs are not peculiar to the later years.
For this reason, therefore, it is evident that the definition of the
Third Age brings with it implicit challenges to established
conventions about the relationships between chronological age,
education, occupation, and social status, across the whole life
course.

Michel Philibert explained in chapter 3 that 'Université du
Troisième Age' was first proposed by Prof. Pierre Vellas, of the
Université des Sciences Sociales in Toulouse, in 1973. As well
as a lecture and seminar programme, Vellas was also interested
in the opportunity for research, particularly socio-medical
research relating to the vitality of life in the later years, with
which those enrolled in the programme could co-operate.
Initially there was nothing exceptional about this programme,
apart from the fact that one section of a large provincial French

university had taken an interest in the problems of ageing, and decided to enlist the resources of the whole university in a programme for senior citizens which would at the same time provide some returns in helping to define the needs of older persons. What is important is that the initiative in Toulouse struck a rich vein of motivation, with the result that this local, provincial, summer experiment was taken over by the student body of senior citizens and parlayed into a year-round programme. More than this, it immediately became the seed-bed from which the concept was disseminated across France and internationally.

From the summer of 1973 in Toulouse the proliferation of the U3A concept has been quite phenomenal. The idea quickly crossed international frontiers. Already by 1975 there were beginnings of U3A programmes in Belgium, Switzerland, Poland, Italy, Spain, the U.S.A., and Quebec in Canada. In that year, as a result of discussions held at Charleroi in Belgium in 1974, an International Association of the Universities of the Third Age (IAU TA) was founded at a congress in Toulouse, and since then annual congresses have been held in different centres; Lille 1976, Toulouse 1977, Namur (Belgium) 1978, Nancy 1979, Sherbrooke (Canada) 1980, Madrid (Spain) 1981, Nice 1982, and Riva Del Garda (Italy) 1983.

It is interesting to note that it was not until December 1980 that any national organisation was established in France. In that year the Union Francaise des Universités du Troisième Age (U.F.U.T.A.) was founded, under the presidency of Prof. Rene Frentz of Nancy, and with a secretariat hosted by the M.G.E.N. Club des Retraités de la Région Parisienne, under the care of M. Pierre Brasseul, as first Secretary-General. In striking contrast to the normal French tradition in education, therefore, the U3A movement in France has been not only primarily provincial and decentralised, but it has also had strong international tendencies from its inception. This aspect leads one to ask whether or not there is something particular in the U3A's character which is a challenge to French educational traditions, which thus contributes to the patently self-conscious sense of innovation in the U3A, and to the movement's vitality.

The U3A is rightly described as an idea and a movement. In France each centre is a local foundation and a uniquely local variant of the theme. Some have been established as separate constituents of an established University (Centres, Institutes, or Colleges), and others came about through association between a university and a government or municipal department responsible for the welfare of older persons. Several are the direct creations not of a university but of local government, and the allocation of funds to such an institution has been featured in local government elections. Some, and of these Grenoble is a prime example, are wholly independent associations. Michel Philibert himself, from his base at the Centre Pluridisciplinaire de Gérontologie, was a prime mover in the introduction of the idea in Grenoble in January 1976, but the U3A is self-directed, and in effect negotiates with the various university centres in the town for the programmes it wishes to set up. In Paris, the programme at Nanterre (Paris X) is an integral part of the University under the tutelage of the Institut d'Education Permanente, but at the same time it had an agreement by which it assisted in programmes negotiated by the M. G. E. N. Club des Retraités (a retired teachers' association). However, in late 1983 there were changes in the M. G. E. N. organisation which have closed this particular programme.

While this diversity of structure, and of financial support and resources, permits the kind of flexibility which allows for a proliferation of centres, there is considerable concern not only for stability and security, but also for credibility. Indeed one of the problems faced by the U. F. U. T. A. in 1980 at its formation, and since then, has been the definition of what qualifies for membership, and what kinds of programmes and organisations are eligible to become members. It is indeed a very touchy question, tempering the enthusiasm which has led to such a rapid proliferation with concern that the good news should not be compromised. In 1983 U. F. U. T. A. counted thirty-one members, with programmes established in some one hundred and thirty centres. The Union also noted a further sixteen institutions which had taken the name U3A, but which did not belong, either by choice or because they did not meet the statutory requirements of the Union. These requirements appear to turn on a debate over the meaning of the word 'Université'. In a report prepared for the Assises Nationales des Retraités et Personnes Agées held in Paris in March 1983 M. Jean Peuziat identifies three broad areas of activity that make up the mission of the U3A: instruction, productive research, and personal development. While recognising the diversity of previous educational achievement among those who participate, and holding to the principle that the qualification for entry should be defined by personal motivation, however, he argues that, 'Nevertheless, in order to preserve the credibility of the label 'University', it is desirable to increase the proportion of university faculty instructors, in order to qualify for resources appropriate to universities.' Prof. René Frentz of Nancy, in his opening address to the first national conference of U. F. U. T. A., in September 1981, also noted the principle of the Union that all members should have a

direct link ('lien organique réel') with a recognised and
established university.

This in effect poses again the issue, raised earlier in the
chapter, of the U3A as in some measure an expression of a
counter-culture, the resort of those to whom a fair measure of
educational opportunity has been denied. Again to quote M.
Peuziat there are claims 'such as this phrase from a worker
who had quit school at twelve years: "The State owes me four
years of schooling".' It is from this well-spring of interest
that we find in France as the movement grew a tendency to
broaden and qualify the name: Universite du Troisième Age
et des Temps Disponsible (and of uncommitted time) at Nancy,
Université du milieu de la vie (of the middle years) et du
Troisième Age of the Institut Catholique in Paris, Université du
Troisième Age et pour tous (and for all) at St Etienne, Université
Tous Ages (all ages) at Lyons, Centre Universitaire Interâges
(intergenerational) at Grenoble, and Université Populaire du
Troisième Age at Mulhouse. The list of formulations could be
extended, but the message and implications are clear. The U3A
is not only significant for the elderly, it is also quite consciously,
in France at least, a challenge in support of the right to life-long
education. Indeed the first demand of the Peuziat report
referred to above, in its summary of propositions, is 'that there
should be solemn recognition at the highest level of State authority,
in a declaration and in official documents, of the right of all
citizens to benefit throughout the life-course from permanent
education adapted to their needs and their capacities.' When we
come to the second demand in this document, which places a
peculiar responsibility on the established Universities to support
what is posed as a recasting ('refonte') of the whole structure of
education, we begin to catch a sense of the belief among some
adherents that the U3A has undertaken no less than a Promethean
task of bringing fire from Olympus.

(B) U3As: The Worldwide Movement
It is important to appreciate something of the quality of the movement as it has developed in France, in order to assess its role
and impact in other countries. The term 'University' does not
necessarily carry the same meaning or definition of role and
organisation in all societies. And even where the institutions
themselves may be broadly similar in organisation and function,
there may be considerable differences in social perceptions and
aspirations, in accessibility and opportunity. One must ask
whether, even if this phenomenon is 'the answer' to a French
question, it is equally the answer to a need which is perceived

in another society. Nevertheless it is significant that the
International Association of the Universities of the Third Age
predated U. F. U. T. A. by six years, and that by 1983, ten years
after its inception, the Association counted some one hundred and
ten institutions established in Argentina, Belgium, Britain, Canada,
France, West Germany, Italy, Poland, Spain, Sweden, Switzerland and the U. S. A. This does not exhaust the list of countries,
which it would be hard to document, where there are, as in France,
institutions which have taken inspiration from the concept and are
even using the name but which for one reason or another have not
formally applied for membership in I. A. U. T. A; even distant
countries such as Japan, China and Ghana.

It will be evident from the imprecision of the count that the
concept of establishing a University of the Third Age outreaches
the grasp not only of the Union Française but also of the International Association too, but while this may suggest a certain
laxity of definition of precisely what the phenomenon is, it is at
the same time evidence that the idea strikes a responsive chord
in a wide variety of communities. At the same time, as we cross
international boundaries, we merge paths and travel together with
other models such as programmes for seniors in the Scandinavian
Folk High Schools, Elderhostel in the U. S. A., and programmes
such as Birmingham's FIR-cone or the Bedford Retirement
Education Centre in the U. K. This is dictated necessarily not
only by social and cultural variations, but also by the administrative and legal differences between different national provisions for
the establishment and funding of adult education programmes, and
by local laws which govern the formation of popular associations.

Nevertheless, before examining some of the different ways in
which U3A outside of France have come into being, it is worth
noting the basic similarities which unite them. Charlotte Nusberg,
writing on educational opportunities for the elderly in industrialised
countries, in Educational Gerontology (Vol. 8, No. 1, July-August
1982), has identified a list of common characteristics which seem
to represent the objectives of organisations participating in the
international U3A movement. These are: (i) programmes to
'enhance older persons' mental and physical well-being and ward
off the symptoms that can occur with aging', (ii) stimulation of
'older persons' social contacts with both their age peers and other
age groups', (iii) the democratisation of education 'by reaching
out to groups that have been neglected by universities in the past,
such as the elderly', (iv) 'to raise the social consciousness of
older students and make them more militant on their own behalf',
(v) 'to seek to stimulate their students to participate more
actively in the life around them through volunteer work of various

kinds and involvement in other community activities', and (vi)
'to be responsive to local needs and interests.' This last
objective is particularly significant in countries which had been
accustomed to a more superimposed, centralised and directive
tradition in educational programming.

The majority of U3A outside of France appear to have developed on a local basis, usually at the initiative of an individual
associated with a university who has heard of the concept and sees
it as a solution to problems which have already been locally
identified. The Université du Troisième Age, in such cases, gave
a name, and perhaps in some cases a degree of focus to proposals
that were already in the process of formulation. This, obviously
enough, was the case with the initiative in Britain. The desire to
promote new programmes specifically for older persons, going
significantly beyond what was already available, had been con-
verging towards definition for several years before this. Already
a wholly indigenous movement had become focussed by Age Concern,
the Centre for Policy on Ageing, Help the Aged, The National
Institute of Adult and Continuing Education, the Pre-Retirement
Association, and other interests in the formulation of F. R. E. E.
(the Forum of the Rights of the Elderly to Education) in 1980.
It is even more difficult to say precisely what the idea of a
University of the Third Age, though elegantly presented by
Michel Philibert with due regard for British sensitivities towards
a French concept, has added to this wholly indigenous fermentation
of ideas. Perhaps this is the genius of Piere Vellas, not to have
invented a new model, but quite simply to have given a name to an
idea whose time had come, not only in Toulouse, but simultaneously in many other places too. This has been called the 'Aha
effect! '

Britain is a comparative latecomer to the movement. For
obvious reasons it was quick to be heard of in the Francophone
world. In Belgium at Charleroi in 1975, Prof. Serge Mayence of
the Institut Européen Inter-universitaire de l'Action Sociale
established a programme that was soon emulated at Tournai,
Mons, Nivelles and La Louvière. Prof. Mayence became the
second president of the International Association in 1978. In 1980
the presidency passed to Prof. Roger Bernier of Canada, who had
been active in establishing programmes at his own Université de
Sherbrooke, Quebec, from where the idea was carried to Hull and
Victoriaville both in Quebec, and Moncton, New Brunswick. So
far no Anglophone Canadian centres have associated with the movement, though the name has in part been adopted by T. A. L. A., the
Third-Age Learning Association, founded by Mrs Janet McPhee,
herself a senior student, in 1979, and based at Glendon College

Campus of York University in Toronto. T. A. L. A. is not itself
a University of the Third Age, though Glendon's programmes
would qualify, but an association analogous to FREE in the UK.
T. A. L. A. has national aspirations but is presently primarily
active in Ontario.

In Spain the movement took a more directive approach. In
June 1978 Sr. Francisco Garrido Verdu, Director of the Institute
Superior de Complemento de Estudios, Valladolid, was charged
by the Director-General for Community Development of the
Ministry of Culture with the task of developing a plan for the
introduction of the U3A concept across the country. In September
of the same year the Ministry signed agreements with appropriate
institutions in twenty-one major population centres for the
establishment of 'Aulas de Tercera Edad.' As a result, and in
contrast with all other cases, Spain is unique in being able to show
a co-ordinated approach summarised in an impressive document
describing in detail, and centre by centre, the establishment of
the national system, in its first year (Aulas de Tercera Edad,
Memoria, Curso 1978-79, Ministerio de Cultura, Madrid 1980).

The Spanish system, for that is indeed the proper word for this
case, was planned and put into operation in consultation with Prof.
Vellas, and the twenty-one original centres plus three more added
subsequently joined the International Association en bloc at the
Congress of Nancy in 1979. Spain even offers a basic 'elemental'
definition, or statement of purpose, which may be worth quoting:
'The Aulas de Tercera Edad are sociocultural centres where
senior citizens may acquire new knowledge of significant issues,
or validate the knowledge which they already possess, in an
agreeable milieu and in accordance with easy and acceptable
methods, with the objective of preserving their vitality and
participating in the life of the community.' It may be argued
that the Spanish system seems to be in distinct contradiction to
the principle of local initiative which informs the movement in
other countries. To a degree this is true, but it must be pointed
out that in Spain this comes at a time when the whole educational
system is undergoing a significant and sweeping reformulation
introduced by the national policy document La Educacion en
España; Bases para una política educativa, 1969. This document,
Spain's first real educational reform in over a century, incorpor-
ates much of the latest thought on life-long education, and is
itself a significant attempt to democratise education and make it
a matter of public and popular responsibility. It is indeed a recasting of the system of the dimensions called for by the
U. F. U. T. A. in France. While it is yet too soon to see how well
the implementation of these educational reforms will progress in

Spain, given the political and social adjustments that are taking place in the post-Franco years, it would be fair to argue that in principle and in theory, in Spain more than anywhere, the Ministry of Education is formally committed to a course of development which is quite consonant with the standard U3A model, and is therefore giving it a fair wind. Certainly a perusal of the resulting programmes in local centres and the organisational structures that have come into being through this Ministry initiative suggests that the process is very similar to what is happening in other countries, in terms of local involvement.

With such a rapid proliferation it would be difficult to complete an exhaustive list of U3As, particularly since, as has been pointed out, the adoption of the term tends to outrun formal affiliation with the Association. Italy should be mentioned as one of the earlier associates of the movement, with centres in Florence, Rome, Turin, Milan and Trento. Professor Antonini, holder, since 1957, of the first Italian chair in Gerontology, at the University of Florence, has been active in I. A. U. T. A. since 1975. In 1982 he established the Universita di Tempo Libero, an all-age institution sponsored by the University and the City of Florence. The USA also has shown interest with seven centres including the Harvard Institute for Learning in Retirement, and the Institute for Retired Professionals in New York. Two of the USA programmes, in San Diego and at the University of Missouri at Rolla, have adopted the name University of the Third Age. As an example, the University of Missouri at Rolla, which in 1977 was the first in the USA to import the name, operates a U3A programme through five campus centres, at Rolla, Columbia, Kansas City, St Louis, and Jefferson City, and each of these five centres services three satellites within its own twenty-five miles radius. This programme was initiated by the University's Center for Aging Studies, very appropriately, for the Ozark region which claims the highest density of older persons in the States, after Florida.

Of particular interest, in view of the social and political issues that have exercised the country recently, is the U3A movement in Poland. Prof. Helena Swarc of the Post-Diploma Medical Centre of the University of Warsaw met Prof. Vellas at a conference of gerontologists in Milan in April 1975. In October that year she obtained permission from its Director to make use of Centre facilities to develop a Universytet III Wieku. Following a successful first year, the University joined the I. A. U. T. A. in 1976, and in the same year a sister institution opened in Wroclaw. Initially the programmes depended on aid in time given by teachers, and in space from institutions of higher learning, but in 1978 a

grant-in-aid was received from the Ministry of Health and
Social Welfare. New centres were opened in Posnan, Szczecin
and Opolu, and in subsequent years further centres have been
created in Gdansk, Lodz, Krakow, Katowice and Gliwice. The
Polish movement has actively promoted the idea at conferences
in other Eastern European countries and the USSR, although at
this time the only specific case of adoption seems to be the
Seniors' University sponsored by Humboldt University in Berlin.
However Poland seems to see itself as having a special mission
in mediating the concept from west to east. The programmes of
the Polish U3A show an interesting blend of Polish cultural
patriotism, exemplified in inaugural addresses that tend to
highlight major themes and events in Polish history, with an
earnest internationalism that cultivates and cherishes the
opportunity of links with other members of the association,
through the teaching of foreign languages (a choice of eighteen in
Warsaw in 1982) and literature. There is also a strong emphasis
on social and medical research into the conditions of an active
and healthy third age. The events of 1981-82 caused a temporary
suspension of activities from December to February, but the
programme returned vigorously in 1982-83.

In a short period the idea of a University of the Third Age has
gained not only international recognition, but also, and perhaps
more importantly, local meaning for many elderly persons who
want (to quote the title of a Beth Johnson Foundation publication
that cannot be bettered) something 'Beyond Bingo and
Condescension'. On the international scene the International
Association of the Universities of the Third Age has become a
recognised Non-Governmental Organisation (NGO) with accredi-
tation to the United Nations, UNESCO, WHO, the Council of
Europe and the European Parliament. It has a permanent
Secretariat at the University of Toulouse, and its own Document-
ation Centre at the European Interuniversity Institute for Social
Action, at Marcinelle, in Belgium. Locally, the concept seems
to have given effective impetus and outlet to a growing demand
among older persons for the recognition of educational rights and
the creation of educational opportunities. It is true that there
are limitations, one of which seems to be a social class bias
which is conditioned by the patterns of educational opportunity
previously prevailing. The U3A initially attracts those who have
had at least secondary education, and many who have had a
university education. Typically, as is the case in adult education,
those who receive are those who have had some before. But these
are encouraging signs that in seeing its role as a special response
to a particular kind of educational deprivation, the movement has

identified a primary issue of educational imbalance. Research programmes in many centres, conducted by the elderly themselves, which are trying to identify the causes and clarify the issues of the loss of social status in the Third Age, illustrate the fact that chronological age itself is a characteristic but not a necessary determining factor. Therefore they contribute to a new perception of forces which govern inequality of educational opportunity, and contribute to a restructuring of education that challenges not only ageist stereotypes but also other impediments to a learning society.

Chapter 5

SELF-HELP LEARNING AND ITS RELEVANCE FOR LEARNING AND DEVELOPMENT IN LATER LIFE

PAULA ALLMAN

Dr. Paula Allman is Course Tutor for the Diploma in Adult
Education and lectures in Adult Developmental Psychology at
the University of Nottingham. She came to the United Kingdom
from the United States in 1973 and has also worked for the
Open University. Both her research and practical work is
focussed on the psycho-social aspects of ageing and its relation to group self-directed learning.

Paula Allman begins from the now accepted, if scarcely
popularly believed, proposition that 'an adult's age has
nothing to do with his or her ability to learn'. She then
analyses the learning processes of an educational approach
with which she has been primarily concerned and which she
claims is an alternative to traditional 'pedagogics', with its
emphasis on the acquiring of knowledge and skills. Paula
Allman's positive insistence on a collective process of
dialogue and reflection in the 'peer learning group' and her
admirable recognition of the potential of adults 'to exercise
control over their own learning' offers the 'mutual aid
university' its own psychological rationale. The plea by
Michael Young for the liberation of people to determine their
own actions, often in co-operative ventures; Peter Laslett's
requirement that U3A members should teach, or otherwise
help, as well as learn; Michel Philibert's yearning for adults
perpetually un-learning, de-learning and re-learning; all
these strands are touched by, and in turn touch, Paula Allman's
belief in and justification of self-help learning.

More so than other chapters, this one of its nature quotes from
a series of learned sources. These are alluded to by author's
name and date, and the full list of references is appended to
the end chapter in alphabetical order.

I would expect that everyone who reads this book shares the

belief that an adult's age has nothing to do with his or her ability to learn. Some readers will hold that belief because they have witnessed their own experience while others will have observed the experiences of the growing numbers of older people who are continuing their learning and doing so just as effectively as their younger counterparts. These beliefs and observations have received substantive support from the past decade of American (Schaie, 1975; Labouvie-Vief) and British (Huppert, 1982) research which has so aptly demonstrated that there is no valid evidence of inevitable decline in learning ability with age.

Of course the ability to learn, at any age, depends upon one's ability to think, or what psychologists call cognitive or intellectual aptitude. During the 1970s, research into ageing and intellectual aptitude was conducted according to approaches which improved upon many of the faults which were inherent in previous research designs. The results of that research helped to dispel 'the myth of intellectual or cognitive decline' in the later years - at least the myth was purged from the thinking of most psychologists. Unfortunately, amongst the public in general, a negative stereotype of ageing persists. This is partly because many people still confuse unhealthy or pathological ageing (which only affects a small minority of older people) and healthy ageing. The resilience of the negative image of age is maintained by a variety of social and psychological factors not the least of which is our own personal fear of ageing and eventual death. If we could lay our stereotypical thinking about ageing aside and with it our fears of ageing, we would discover that whether a person is declining or progressing at any age depends on his or her health and on the degree to which and the quality with which a person interacts with other people and with ideas and issues - in other words the interaction of people with the total social and historical context in which they live.

This chapter is only indirectly related to the previously mentioned research which I have discussed in full elsewhere (Allman, 1981, 1982). I have mentioned it so that readers might be assured that their belief in older people's learning potential is a sound one. I have also referred to that research because it has led to the serious study of adult psychological development which has in turn begun to revolutionise our thinking about adulthood. It is this relatively new and very exciting branch of psychological study which has the most to say to us about learning and development during the adult years. And I hope to show that what it says points very clearly to the appropriateness and extreme relevance of the self-help learning process during the later years of life.

(A) The Importance of Experience in Adult Thought and the
     Nature of Adult Development

Prior to the late 1970's our study of adulthood was stymied by the
fact that most of our concepts, theories and ideas about thinking
or intellectual/cognitive aptitude were derived from the study of
children and adolescents. Coupled with a social and legal system
that recognizes the advent of maturity sometime towards the end
of adolescence, we were left with the dual notions that adults were
developed, ie. mature, and that, with reference to their thinking
abilities, we could expect adults to be capable of thinking like a
fully developed or mature adolescent.

Accoring to child and adolescent developmental psychology,
this mature thought, or the processes of which mature thought is
constituted, conform to the model of formal or propositional
logic (Piaget, 1972). Thinking with formal logic involves being
able to disassociate the processes of thought from the content of
thought: therefore, one becomes capable of abstract thinking.
It also involves being able to deduce the variables from a given
problem and systematically, that is, by instituting controls, to
test each variable and each combination of variables until a
solution to the problem is reached. For example, a typical
Piagetian test of formal thinking would be to ask someone to
determine what factor or factors cause the velocity of a pendulum's
swing. To solve this problem one must deduce which variables
might be involved, such as the length of the string, the height
from which the weight is dropped, the variation in possible weights.
Each variable must be tested in isolation and in combination with
all other variables held constant until the correct solution is
derived. It is the process used to arrive at the correct solution
which the psychologist focusses upon rather than the solution or
correct answer, because the process implies the underlying
thought structure or stage of cognitive development.

A great deal of research into the extent of formal operational
thought amongst adult had indicated that this type of thinking, was
not very prevalent amongst adult (Papalia and Bielby, 1974).
Piaget had not studied adults but when asked to reflect upon these
findings he noted (Piaget, 1972) that adults would probably only
display formal thought on problems for which they had an
aptitude. Therefore if we can assume a connection between
aptitude and the types of experience an adult seeks out in work
and leisure, it is in problems of this sort that we would be more
likely to find adults employing thinking according to a model of
formal logic. Sinnott (1975) confirmed this hypothesis when he
derived a series of problems which, whilst demanding formal
logic, were framed within content pertinent to typical adult life

74

experiences. In fact Piaget himself had hinted at the importance of experience in a much earlier discussion of adolescence.

> '.... Adolescent egocentricity is manifested by a belief in the omnipotence of reflection, as though the world should submit itself to idealistic schemes rather than to systems of reality...... so the metaphysical egocentricity of the adolescent is gradually lessened as a reconcilation between formal thought and reality is effected.'
> (Piaget, 1967, pp. 63-64)

About the same time that we began to recognize the importance of experience to adult thinking, psychologists began to question whether other types of thinking structures might develop during adulthood and whether experience might not change the nature of formal logic in some manner so as to render it qualitatively more adaptive in terms of functioning effectively as a mature adult.

I shall attempt to describe chronologically the research and theoretical responses to these questions and to offer a tentative model of the types of thinking which can develop during the adult years as well as a model for the process of adult development. Any such model must be tentative for two reasons. Firstly, the concerted study of adulthood has only just begun in relative terms. And, secondly, we now recognize that the potential for development during adulthood is inter-related with individuals' interactions with a social and historical context which is itself dynamic. Therefore as a consequence of social and historical change people may need to develop progressively adaptive ways of thinking. Nevertheless this tentative model points to some clear implications for adult learning which seriously challenge some of our traditional assumptions and practices of adult education.

Arlin (1975) was the first to offer research results which challenged our traditional notions about the adults' thinking potential. The results of her study revealed that the ability to ask or discover important questions develops subsequent to the stage of formal operation which results in deriving the answers to questions and solutions to problems. Neugarten's research (1977) into middle-aged people's thinking strategies identified an increasing use of reflective thinking. Whereas Moshman's (1979) study suggested that what he labelled 'metatheoretical thought', or the ability to think about one's own theories and processes of theorising, also develops subsequent to formal operational thought. All of these studies can be linked to a point that Piaget made in some of his later writings which can be taken as a

hypothesis that other forms of thought will emerge from formal
operational thinking, namely, that what constitutes the form of
thought at one stage of development becomes the content of
thought during the next progressive adaptation (Piaget, 1970).

The most interesting and well developed theory of adult
cognitive development was first proposed by Klaus Riegel in 1973
and was subsequently developed by him throughout most of the
1970s (Riegel, 1979). Riegel proposed a model of adult thinking
based on the system of dialectic logic. In so doing, he was not
denying that some adult thinking can be characterised by the
formal logic model. However, according to Riegel, dialectic
logic is much more characteristic of effective adult thinking; and
therefore it provides a better model of the adult's potential for
development than does formal logic which is more appropriately
related to the adolescent's potential for development. The
previously mentioned studies by Arlin, Neugarten and Moshman
can be linked to one or another aspect of dialectic operational
thought; therefore, they offer an indirect source of support for
this very important theory.

Dialectic operations can be best explained by comparing and
contrasting the processes involved in this type of thinking with
those involved in formal operational thought.

The theory of dialectic locic or dialectic operational thought
depicts a type of thinking which results in the discovery of
important questions and problems. This demands the abilities
to tolerate contradictions and to use the tension between two or
more contradictory explanations as a creative force which allows
for the discovery of new questions and problems. Whereas formal
operational thought involves the elimination of contradiction in
order to solve problems or to answer questions. In the process
of dialectic thinking, abstract thought, or ideas and concepts, are
reunited with concrete reality and experience. And it is from
this reunion that contradictions emerge and become the dynamic
or motivational forces for dialectic thinking. In other words, not
only are contradictions tolerated by the dialectic thinker but
they also excite or energize the thinking process.

When we think according to the system of formal logic, we
attempt to isolate the 'identity' of an object, ie. it is this and not
that. However when we think dialectically we can also recognize
that objects are this and yet not this. A very simple example
would be the identification of large or big. At a certain age a
child can easily distinguish large objects from small ones. This
process pertains to a stage in the development of formal logic.
However in dialectical thought the context becomes important and
one is able to recognize the relativity of classification schemes;

for instance, what is large or big within one context may not be large or big within another context.

This does not mean that answers or points of stability never result in the course of dialectic thinking, but when they do they are resting points, temporary resolutions rather than immutable structures or final causes. Riegel contends that the most effec- tive adult thinking and the type of thinking which fosters develop- ments in scientific thought and human relations is not that which provides the immediate answer but that which discovers the important question or poses an important problem. (Riegel, 1978). Of course the mature adult thinker would be capable of formal operational thought and this type of thinking is often useful and effective for certain types of problem solving activities. However dialectic thought is not only more important within the adult's life experience but is demanded more because of the complex nature of the vast majority of that experience. Whether or not an adult interacts with these complex experiences according to the model of dialectic thought is another matter. Riegel's theory predicts the _potential_ for mature adult thought, and therefore it is not necessarily a description of how all or most adults think within the total context of their experiences.

There are several factors which may act as barriers to the development and use of dialectic thinking. Not the least of these is the tendency for our society to conceive of thinking within the framework of formal logic. These conceptions are reflected in the institutional structures and objectives of our educational system and are also mirrored in our popular notions of the intelligent or educated person. The educated person is normally. envisioned as one who can solve problems or deliver answers not one who discovers problems and questions. It is my opinion, however, that there is a pull or force exerted when an adult becomes interactive with his/her life experiences that helps the person to transcend the traditional forms of thinking. Some people may experience this development fairly early in adulthood but others, due to the nature of their interactions with adult life experience, may not undergo further development until quite late in life. And, unfortunately, some may never experience it given the present barriers imposed by our societal notions of thinking and education. There are other barriers as well, some of which we shall touch upon in our discussion of learning styles.

The research and theory mentioned to this point deal directly with cognitive or thinking development. There is one more piece of very recent research in this context with which I would like to deal before discussing two other areas of adult developmental research which have added indirect support to Riegel's theory of of dialectic operations. Moshman, Neugarten, Arlin, and Riegel have addressed the question of the nature of adult thinking potential, that is, the structures and related processes which characterise effective or mature adult thought and which distinguish it from the thought of the mature adolescent. Labouvie-Vief (1980) has focussed her attention on the process of development during the adult years and has suggested a fundamentally different model of that process than the one we had assumed on the basis of Piaget's theory of child and adolescent development.

According to Piaget's theory, development proceeds in a stage sequence which is hierarchial in nature. Each stage is structurally more advanced than the proceeding one and the sequence is universal and invariant: everyone should pass through the same stages in the same order, though not necessarily at the same age. Stage theories of development have led to a 'last in-first out' model of development in adulthood because psychologists assumed that, when and if cognitive decline occurred in old age, it would do so in an order which was the reverse of the order of acquisition. A variety of research into the effects of age on cognitive functions supported this model in the past. However, Labouvie-Vief pointed out that one of the problems with that research was that psychologists were using tests or instruments derived from child and adolescent psychology; therefore the abilities under review were those we expected in the course of adolescent maturation. For example, in the vast majority of research into memory the type of memory being tested was memory for detail. Labouvie-Vief and colleagues devised alternative instruments designed to reveal higher order memory abilities, such as, memory for concepts, gist and principles. When tested with these instruments older adults performed as well as and sometimes even out performed their younger counterparts. As a consequence, Labouvie-Vief has suggested a 'first in-first out' or 'trade-off' model of the developmental process. This means that as we develop during the adult years we may have to shed or trade off abilities acquired at an earlier age in order to acquire abilities which are more advanced or more relevant to the demands of adult life experience. Whether or not we truly jettison the early abilities or simply fail to display them because of preference for others or because they are used so infrequently remains a question. However this developmental process model fits nicely with, and reaffirms, the ideas about the potential for progressive adaptations in the quality of adult thinking which we discussed earlier.

Research into adult moral development and the adult learner's relationship to his/her learning has also borne witness to the

development of qualitatively different ways of thinking during the
adult years. And in both cases the apex of maturity would appear
to involve dialectical rather than formal reasoning.

In the study of moral development, Kohlberg's theory,
(Kohlberg, 1976) which was derived from Piaget's theory of
cognitive development, has figured most prominently. This is a
stage theory in which the highest stages of moral reasoning require
formal logic as a necessary though not sufficient condition.
Researching within the Kohlberg tradition, Gilligan and Murphy
(1979) have discovered a qualitative transformation in adults'
moral reasoning. Their research differed from previous studies
because they had the advantage of studying a group over a period
of seven years. Their subjects had responded to Kohlberg-type
moral dilemmas or problems in a study which was conducted
whilst the subjects were college students. Every member of the
group which was studied by Gilligan and Murphy had been assessed
as reasoning at a post-conventional or highly principled stage of
moral reasoning during the initial study. After seven years and
numerous adult life experiences, Gilligan and Murphy asked their
subjects to look at their original responses to the problems and
to say what they thought about them. The responses after the
seven year period reflected a developmental evolution from the
perfection of formal logic as a basis for moral reasoning through
to the placement of this reasoning 'within the broader context of
a more differentiated and dialectical understanding' of the
problem (p. 91).

> Our data is compatible with the interpretation that this
> discovery (ie. of the consequences of moral reasoning through
> logical justification) requires a cognitive transformation
> from a formal to a dialectical model of reasoning that can
> encompass the contradictions out of which moral problems
> themselves arise. While formal logic and principles of
> justice can release adolescent judgement from the binding
> constraints of a conventional mode of moral reasoning, the
> choices that arise in adulthood impose a new context for
> moral decisions that changes the dimensions of the problem
> ..... These transformations arise out of the recognition
> of the paradoxical interdependence of self and society
> which overrides the false simplicity of formal reason
> and replaces it with a more encompassing form of judgement.
> (Gilligan and Murphy, p. 97)

In other words, the adolescent may be able to formulate a logically
reasoned or highly principles response to a problem by focussing

on a single context or concept such as truth or justice. However, the mature adult will also have to consider the consequences of applying the principle which will introduce other contexts for consideration, such as the rights of others. Mature moral reasoning, therefore, is characterised by multiple contexts and, as a consequence, can encompass or deal with the contradictions which produce the moral problem.

Gilligan and Murphy's approach to their research was influenced by Perry's (1970) research into the relationship between a learner and his or her learning. In his extended study of Harvard undergraduates, Perry had found that this relationship developed through a nine stage squence which can be simplified into three categories or ways of relating to knowledge. In the early stages of university or higher education, learners adopt an absolutistic or dualistic stance which is reflected in their belief that 'the truth' exists and can be found; therefore there are answers which are right and those which are wrong. Later the learner recognizes that knowledge and authoritative explanations of phenomena are relative and contextually dependent. Ultimately, however, whilst the learner's thought remains within the context of relativism, it is reunited with affectivity, and commitment to particular explanations develops. This last category which includes stages 7, 8 and 9 in Perry's scheme would appear to entail dialectical reasoning and therefore a qualitative transformation of thought (together with a qualitative change in the learner's relationship to learning) can potentially develop during early adulthood. Whether or not dialectical thought and its related modes of learning are displayed in adults will depend to a considerable extent on the learning context, including the approach or educational learning style as well as the educator's educational philosophy and consequent objectives.

Before turning to the educational implications which we can derive from this research and theory, I would like to summarise by proposing a concept or model of the adult's developmental potential. Paulo Freire (1972) talks about the human vocation or the humanising process as being one of movement from being 'adapted' or controlled by knowledge or myths to being 'intergrated' or conscientised and therefore in control of one's own knowledge and thought. He goes on to say that control is achieved through critical reflection and action. It seems to me that all of the research so far discussed has to do with adults' potential to acquire greater control over their thinking, action and feeling. It is thought in interaction with experience which leads to this control. For example, adolescent reflection is abstract and alienated from experience; less so, of course, as

adolescence proceeds. Therefore, it may well be that reflection
in adulthood is not just increasing, as Neugarten (1977) suggests,
but is qualitatively transformed by the reunion of thought and
experience. Mature reflection and reasoning encompass multiple
contexts and, as a consequence, contradictions, and, if Riegel
is correct, this dialectical complexity energizes and excites
creative and effective adult thought. The direction of our developmental potential, during the adult years, therefore, is one of
increasing control and self-direction of our thinking, our feeling
and our actions.

(B) The Educational Implications: the Andragogic Approach
The educational implications which can be derived from the
emerging theory of adult developmental potential are profoundly
important and this is especially true if we consider the present
campaign for the rights of older people to education. Most ardent
campaigners, be they young, middle-aged or old, have assumed
that education during the later years is important for keeping an
already developed mind active. An active mind is less likely to
suffer the perils of age even in cases where physical impairment
is present. Of course others argue for the older person's
educational rights because of social factors such as missed
opportunities at a younger age. Nevertheless, most if not all
campaigners are centrally concerned with the benefits that can
be derived from mental activity. However, if this were the only
purpose or objective, it would seem to me to make little difference
to a motivated learner which educational approach or learning
style is employed. If we are simply aiming to maintain a status
quo level of development, all we need to do is to place academic
content and opportunity in the older person's way, and if
motivated he/she will remain mentally active. On the other hand,
if we reconceptualise the purpose of learning during the later
years as having to do with the fulfillment of one's developmental
potential, then, in my opinion, we have seriously to reconsider
not only our approach to education but also our concepts of
education.
   The art and science of teaching is called pedagogy. All forms
of pedagogical practice derive from a common concept of education. According to this conception, the primary objective of
education is to acquire knowledge, ideas and skills. In the
remainder of this chapter, I will propose an alternative approach
to education which derives from the theory and research I have
discussed. This approach is called andragogy or the art and
science of adult learning. One of the most fundamental differences between pedagogy and andragogy has to do with the primary

objectives. Andragogy assumes that learning is synonomous
with thinking rather than acquiring knowledge, ideas and skills.
Therefore the primary objective of an andragogic approach is to
develop progressively more complex ways of thinking. Thinking
about knowledge, ideas and skills places the primary objectives
of pedagogy in a subservient position to thought - they are the
tools of thought and as such new knowledge, ideas and skills can
be created.

During the history of adult education certain styles of learning
or particular modes of practice have evolved which hold a great
deal in common with andragogy. The Swedish study circle and
other forms of self-help learning are good examples. However,
as most proponents of these learning styles will readily admit,
the actual practice frequently falls short of the ideal or philosophical objective. Briefly stated, the ideal is for a group of adults
to exercise control over their own learning. What frequently
happens is that the void created by the absence of the teacher or
authority figure is filled by an influential group member who then
unwittingly creates similar learning/thinking conditions to those
which exist in traditional settings. It was this problem which led
a group of adult education colleagues and myself to spend
considerable time and thinking effort in the systematic formulation of an approach which recognizes the complexity involved in
creating the conditions for realising the commendable aims of the
self-help learning style. (NAG, 1983)

Our 'developmental theory of andragogy' has been influenced
to a considerable degree by our study and dialogue about the
adults' developmental potential and the educational philosophy of
Paulo Freire. The model of the adult's thinking potential depicts
a person in control of their thinking rather than one controlled by
the thinking of others. And Freire's philosophy depicts a process
of education or learning which is one of liberation through a
denunciation of structures which are dehumanising and an announ-
cing of a humanising structure. Dehumanising structures oppress
people in either subtle or direct ways depending upon the historical and cultural context in which they exist: whereas humanising structures are created by people's praxis or that intergra-
tion of thought and action, aimed at, first, the recognition and,
then, the elimination of factors which oppress people. These are
the factors which prevent people from the type of control over
their thought and action which allows them to realise the full
potential of being human. Freire's critique of traditional
education is that it is designed to domesticate or socialise people
into their culture or society. He calls this a 'banking' concept of
education because the teacher's role is to deposit knowledge in the

minds of the learner. Many British educators, whilst admiring Freire's ideas when applied to the Third World context in which they evolved, have seen them as holding little relevance for our own context. However, if Gramsci's concept of hegemony is considered alongside Freire's ideas, then the relevance of Freire to all aspects of adult learning becomes increasingly apparent.

Gramsci's (1971) <u>concept of hegemony</u> explains how societies or cultures develop their own notions of what is 'common sense'. Common sense or hegemony is a vast range of notions which have to do with preserving and guaranteeing the position in society of those who hold the real power. Hegemony is not opposed by those who derive no benefit from it, because even the oppressed accept hegemonic notions as reality or common sense. In emerging nations, or those in a state of upheaval, hegemony is maintained through the military apparatus of the state. Therefore it is more visible or less subtle than it is in mature nation-states, where it is maintained through the apparatus of civil society, such as the media and education.

The practice of pedagogy with adult learners is one example of the subtle influence of 'hegemony' in our society. But because it is subtle it is therefore more complicated to decode than it may have been for Freire and others who were combating much more obvious manifestations of oppression. This is why we would contend that the process of adults coming to control their own thinking and learning will never take place through intent alone. Intent must work in combination with the creation of alternative structures and conditions for learning. Creating alternatives depends primarily on changing the relationship of teacher and learner and the relationship of learners and teachers with knowledge. Freire's ideas inform us as to how we might go about creating both of these changes and this is why they have had such a profound influence on our theory of andragogy.

An andragogic approach to adult learning recognizes that by virtue of being adults both teachers and learners have the potential for further development. Therefore learning is a process wherein adults come together to think, to question and reflect on what they know or on new areas of content, that is, what others think they know, and then to test this against and within experience. In pedagogical approaches to adult learning, be they traditional or progressive, the teacher is always controlling the learning process because he or she determines what the learners should know or discover. In pedagogy, knowledge or authoritative explanation is something the learner needs to acquire. In andragogy, knowledge and authoritative explanation are used in the collective exploration and thinking about a particular problem or question. The problems or questions arise out of the concerns and concrete experiences of the group. Therefore theory and research, within andragogy, is constantly grounded in reality.

Teachers or leaders have only one role in an andragogic learning group that differs from anyone else's role. It is their responsibility to take the initial lead in establishing what we have called a 'peer learning group'. This is neither a simple or automatic process because most of us have only had previous experience of learning pedagogically. Therefore considerable time and effort is needed to decode these experiences and to become conscious of how they serve to impede the development of our full human potential.

With pedagogical approaches there is considerable evidence that learners learn as much if not more from the hidden curriculum than the one encoded in the syllabus. First and foremost, they learn, and then accept or rebel against, the notion that they are incapable of deciding what to learn and how to go about learning it. The andragogical approach makes explicit an alternative notion, viz., that adults are capable of deciding and should decide what to learn and how to learn. Therefore they should be in control of all aspects of their educational experience. Furthermore, they are more likely to realise control over their thinking and their learning if they are involved in each and every aspect of the educational decision making process.

We often dichotomise the educational experience in terms of process versus content. For example, traditional pedagogy is primarily concerned with content and progressive pedagogy with process. Nevertheless, each aims to enable the learner to reach the objectives which the teacher has set. In an andragogic approach to adult learning, process and content are equally important. Not only does the peer learning group share the decision making process with regard to the content and method of learning, but they also share the responsibility for managing the group processes. In andragogy, therefore, the focus is on two types of process: the learning process or method and also the group process or the group dynamics. Negotiation and continuous evaluation or reflection on what is taking place, both in terms of learning or thinking and in terms of relating one to another, are continuous features of andragogic learning.

According to our theory of andragogy, the learning process is primarily a group rather than an individual one. Though it is obviously very complicated for a group to take control over its thinking and learning in this way, it can be argued that the type of development andragogy is aimed at can only be realised through collective effort. In our study of adult development we began to

question whether the kind of thinking which has led to great
advances in science, philosophy or the arts, has ever occurred
through solely isolated or individual problem exploration. Those
to whom we attribute these advances, such as Freud, Marx or
Einstein, share an advantage that most of us do not. Because
they were known to be the 'thinkers' of their time, they shared a
characteristic life style in which serious intellectual dialogue
with others was a constant and common feature. When the human
mind attempts to wrestle with complex problems, the tendency is
to eliminate contradictions and to foreclose on a solution prema-
turely. Thinking through problems collectively can aid in
forestalling such premature closure, but this only happens when
the conditions are created which serve to promote this objective.

While the andragogic approach is centred around problem
posing, this can itself also be thought of as a skill which is an
integral and essential feature within the process of collective
thinking. Within an andragogic approach, collective thinking is
referred to as dialogue. The skill of problem posing can only be
realised within the framework of dialogue. Our concept of
dialogue is a synthesis derived from everything that Freire has
said about dialogue. To our knowledge, there is no one place in
Freire's writings where he describes or explains dialogue in full.
Therefore we have attempted to draw together the various points
that he makes about the process in order to devise a methodology
which enables the development and application of dialectic thought.

In order for a group of people to engage in dialogue, they must
all understand that it is not simply a discussion but a method
designed to enable the development of their most effective thinking.
It is also necessary for the group members initially to value, and
later to reflect through their actions, certain fundamental
assumptions. Dialogue requires people to be engaged in the
process of questioning their existing knowledge. It also requires
them to have a genuine desire to share group member's meanings,
ideas and feelings. Therefore dialogue presupposes attitudes
such as mutual respect and trust of each member for every other
member, so that genuine equality exists within the group experience.
Needless to say this does not transpire fully until openness, trust,
care and commitment have developed within the collective inter-
personal relationships of the group.

Problem posing is a form of communication that is used
within dialogue and which is enabled by dialogue. It differs
considerably from our normal or everyday style of communicating.
In our normal discussions with people we tend to communicate in
a monological as opposed to a dialogical manner. For example,
person A makes a statement and person B responds with a

statement. Sometimes the two statements are related and
sometimes not but whether or not related each is an attempt to
convey personal meaning, explanation or opinion. Dialogic
communication or problem posing requires others to investigate
the meanings, ideas and feelings inherent in each statement that
is communicated, whether it be a statement originating from
within the group or one which the group is considering. Therefore, group members forestall their own immediate responses
and work collectively to question or pose problems which arise
out of the communicated statement. When a group works
collectively to explore each other's thinking, it helps individuals
to question or reflect upon what they know or think they know.
Thus the tendency to 'tell' and, therefore, to oppress or forestall
the collective analysis of the problem is reduced. Since dialogic
communication is not our normal mode of communicating, it
takes a great deal of practice and continuous evaluation in order
to both improve and sustain its development. It is also essential
that all group members share the responsibility for dialogue and
thus share in the problem posing process. If only one or even a
few members take on this responsibility, their thinking will begin
to manipulate or dominate the dialogue, because they will not
have the advantage of the group supporting and helping to sustain
their own critical reflection upon what they think they know.

One further point about dialogue is that it must be grounded
in praxis or the inseparable unity of reflection and action.
Thought in separation from action is also liable to premature
closure. It is only when thought is reunited with action or ongoing experience that it is continually being refined and
developed. According to Freire and according to our own
experience of learning andragogically, these are the conditions
necessary to the creation of knowledge which we deem to be
synonymous with the development of dialectic thought.

I stated earlier that learning experiences during the later
years of life had a potential to do more for an older person than
simply providing mental activity and a maintenance of one's
status quo level of development. I have been arguing that self-
help group learning within an andragogic framework affords the
opportunity for further development and therefore the opportunity
for individuals to realize their full developmental potential. But
I also think there is another opportunity which this style of
learning can offer which may be of equal if not greater importance.
The following quote may help to explain this other opportunity.

As individuals express their life, so they are. What they
are, therefore, coincides with what they produce and how

they produce. The nature of individuals thus depends on
the material conditions which determine their production.
(Karl Marx, with the collaboration of Frederich Engels) The
German Ideology 1846.

Since those words were written, the material conditions of
our society have changed. By and large the material conditions
in our society, have improved. What human beings produce, or
that which they labour to create, takes a variety of forms
including services and knowledge. But the basic tenets, set out
by Marx and Engels in 1846, are still true despite these changes,
because those tenets pertain not only to what is produced, but to
the relationships which exist in the production process and
between the person and what he or she produces. In an educational or learning context, the nature of human beings will
coincide with the quality of the knowledge they produce and both
the nature of the human being and the knowledge created will
coincide with how it is produced; in other words, the relationships between people in the production of knowledge and between
people and knowledge.

An older person in our society today, due to the nature of the
socio-economic organisation of our society, is virtually stripped
of the status and roles which he or she spent the adult years
acquiring. This is because status and roles are primarily
determined by one's position within the economic structure.
Since our structure cannot accommodate the concept of full
employment we have, as a necessity of our system, a surplus
labour force and a retired labour force. Both of these share
many of the same anomalies of this system. When one finds
oneself outside the labour force, one finds that labour, whether
mental or manual, is about filling time or keeping active rather
than being attached to a value of any social or economic
significance.

If, through encouraging learning in the later years, we see
the added opportunity for reallocating some value to people's
mental labour thereby affecting the quality and meaning of their
lives, then we can argue that the way in which learning or
thinking is organised is extremely important. The organisation
of those learning experiences must allow the individual to regain
control over what is produced or created. It follows that not just
any learning experience will achieve all that can be achieved
through promoting learning in the later years. Our experiences
which deal with the fundamental relationships involved in
knowledge production will succeed in returning some degree and
type of value to the older person's life. In learning or educational

contexts, we can only realise the full promise of the experience if we challenge the accepted relationships of teacher and taught and relationship of both of these to knowledge. This is the challenge implicit in the self-help concept of learning; however I have tried to argue that to make the challenge felt as an explicit reality of the learning experience is a complex process. I can only hope that by drawing the reader's attention to the complexity entailed in realising the complete aims of self-help learning that I have not discouraged people from attempting the approach. It is only through attempting, reflecting and attempting yet again that we will begin to work through the complex problems of learning for development and learning for value whether in the later years or during the entirety of adult life.

References

Allman, P. (1981) Adult Development: An Overview of Recent Research No.1 in 'Adults: Psychological and Educational Perspectives' series eds. Allman, P. and Mackie, K., University of Nottingham, Department of Adult Education.

Allman, P. (1982) 'New Perspectives on the Adults: An Argument for Lifelong Education', International Journal of Lifelong Education vol.1, no.1, pp.41-52.

Arlin, P.K. (1975) 'Cognitive Development in Adulthood: A Fifth Stage?' Developmental Psychology, vol.11, pp.602-606.

Freire, P. (1972) Pedagogy of the Oppressed. Harmondsworth: Penguin Books.

Gilligan, C. and Murphy, J.M. (1979) 'Development from Adolescence to Adulthood: The Philosopher and the Dilemma of Fact' in Kuhn, D.(ed) Intellectual Development Beyond Childhood. London: Jossey-Bass, pp.85-99.

Gramsci, A. (1971) The Prison Notebooks. London: Laurence and Wishart.

Huppert, F. (1982) 'Does Mental Function Decline with Age?', Geriatric Medicine, January, pp.32-37.

Kohlberg, L. (1976) 'Moral Stages and Moralization: the Cognitive Developmental Approach' in Lickona, T.(ed) Moral Development and Behaviour. New York: Holt, Rinehart and Winston.

Labouvie-Vief, G. (1977) 'Adult Cognitive Development: In Search of Alternative Interpretations', Merrill-Palmer Quarterly. vol.23, no.4, pp.227-263.

Labouvie-Vief, G. (1980) 'Adaptive Dimensions of Adult Cognition' in Datan, N. and Lohman, N. (eds) Transitions in Aging. London: Academic Press.

Marx, K. with the collaboration of Engels, F. (1846) in McLellan, D. (ed) (1977) Karl Marx; Selected Writings. Oxford University Press.

Moshman, D. (1979) 'To Really Get Ahead, Get a Metatheory', in Kuhn, D. (ed) Intellectual Development Beyond Childhood. London: Jossey-Bass, pp.59-68.

Neugarten, B.L. (1977) 'Adult Personality: Towards a Psychology of the Life-Cycle', in Allman, J.F. and Jaffe, D.T. (eds) Readings in Adult Psychology : Contemporary Perspectives. New York: Harper.

Nottingham Andragogy Group (1983) Towards a Developmental Theory of Andragogy, No.9 in Allman, P. and Mackie, K. (eds) 'Adults: Psychological and Educational Perspectives' series, University of Nottingham, Department of Adult Education.

Papalia, D. E. and Del Vento Bielby, D. (1974) 'Cognitive Functioning in Middle and Old Age Adults: A Review of Research Based on Piaget's Theory', Human Development, 17, pp. 424-443.

Perry, W. I. (1970) Forms of Intellectual and Ethical Development in the College Years : A Scheme. New York: Holt, Rinehart and Winston.

Piaget, J. (1967) Six Psychological Studies. New York: Random House.

Piaget, J. (1970) Structuralism. New York: Basic Books.

Piaget, (1972) 'Intellectual Evolution from Adolescence to Adulthood', Human Development, 16, pp. 1-12.

Riegel, K. (1973) 'Dialectic Operations: The Final Period of Cognitive Development', Human Development, vol. 16, no. 3, pp. 346-370.

Riegel, K. (1978) Psychology Mon Amour: A Counter Text. London: Academic Press.

Riegel, K. (1979) Foundations of Dialectic Psychology. London: Academic Press.

Schaie, K. W. (1975) 'Age Changes in Adult Intelligence', in Woodruff, D. S. and Birren, J. E. (eds) Aging: Scientific Perspectives and Social Issues. New York: D. Van Nostrand.

Sinnott, J. D. (1975) 'Everyday Thinking and Piagetian Operativity in Adults' Developmental Psychology, vol. 18, part 6, pp. 430-443.

Chapter 6

MAJOR INFLUENCES ON U3A DEVELOPMENT

JOHN RENNIE AND MICHAEL YOUNG

Like no man, no idea is an island. It draws inspiration
from other streams of thought and action, and this is
undoubedly true of the U3A notion. Two influences, in
particular, have been paramount. One is community
education. As John Rennie explains, this creed eschews
'the expert-client approach for a collaborative, self-
monitoring and ultimately autonomous one', which, in
turn, is as clear a definition of the U3A mutuality approach
as one could wish. His preference for a 'concentration on
needs identified by the people themselves rather than the
purveying of a pre-determined set of ideas or materials'
is, plainly, the social equivalent of Paula Allman's
andragogic approach. The other influence is the self-help
movement, so firmly identified in Great Britain with
Michael Young, who draws the parallels between the
mutual side of U3A groups and that of a colourful collection
of self-help initiatives from garages and bulk-buying to
health and re-cycling. This illuminates the vital spark
of U3A self-mobilisation, and, importantly, Michael Young
points to the complementary rather than the alternative
character of self-help: 'welfare state and welfare self-help
will flourish together, in partnership'.
John Rennie is Director of the Community Education
Development Centre based on Coventry, where, as
Community Education Adviser, he was chiefly responsible
for that city taking so impressive a lead in this field.
He led the School Council's influential Social Education
Project and is the author, among other material, of
Social Education : An Experiment in Four Secondary
Schools. Under his dynamic leadership, CEDC has
become the vital focus for the expansion of Community
Education in Britain.

Founder of the Consumers' Association, and of the Advisory
Centre for Education, originator of the Open University,
first chairman of the National Consumer Council, president
of the National Extension College .... Michael Young's
record as a social revisionist is without recent parallel.
He was a member of the Plowden Committee and, among
other works, author of the celebrated The Rise of the
Meritocracy. As chairman of both the Mutual Aid Centre
and the University of the Third Age National Committee,
it is appropriate that it is his coinage which provides the
title of this book.

(A) The Community Education Movement   John Rennie
If anything is designed to send shivers down the backs of politicians
and decision-makers, it is the production of statistics showing
large groups of people in some kind of need. Over the last thirty
years, without ever becoming used to it, successive governments
have had to deal with increasingly strident demands for fresh
resources to deal with the newly-awakened aspirations of some
groups or the resigned pleadings of others. Somehow governments survive - despite the forebodings of financially-conscious
ministers and the apocalyptic spectres created by the yellow
press. In turn, it seems, teenagers, ethnic minority groups,
pre-school children, women and the unemployed have smitten the
national consciousness, if not the public conscience, and have
been seen as pressure groups, worthy causes, intolerable burdens
- depending on your political viewpoint.
    Here we are again. In only a year or two, the elderly are
suddenly 'an issue'. Like the teenagers of the late fifties and
early sixties, they are all at once a new market force, a body of
voters to be reckoned with, a focus for media attention. Though
it is hardly surprising that their most clearly articulated needs
have been economic, it has come as something of a shock to note
their revived interest in education. Even more amazing has been
the rapid recognition of their educational needs by professionals
and others in the education service. If this recognition has not
been matched by the provision of funds to meet those needs, nor
the imagination to implement new methods of touching them, then
this is no more than par for the course for the education service.
Since those needs are not going to go away, it behoves that
service to think again - both about funding and about how best to
spend what funds it has.
    It is my purpose to suggest that the most likely way forward
is through community education. What follows is an analysis of
these potential new learners in educational terms; how best to

meet their needs without falling back on the methods which have
palpably failed in the past; and some suggestions as to who will
be the providers and enablers of whatever new provision arises.
i. Who are the New Learners?
More than any other educational characteristic of the elderly the
fact that they are very broadly unqualified is the most potent.
Great advances in secondary, further and higher education after
the second world war came too late for the age-group which is
now either retired or coming up to it. Having gone through the
traumas of that war and the hungry Thirties which preceded it,
they missed out on the educational bonanza (relatively speaking)
which followed it. It would be iniquitous if they were to miss out
again.

The Advisory Council for Adult and Continuing Education has
shown us that only 6% of the over 65's have taken any kind of
course in the preceding three years, as opposed to over 42% of
those aged 25 - 44. We know that only 2 or 3% of LEA adult
education enrolments in 1981-82 were pensioners - despite the
fee-reduction policies of a few enlightened authorities. A massive
80% of the over 65's have no educational qualifications at all.
Whatever talk there is of the undoubted value of the 'school of
hard knocks' and 'the university of life', this is a clear imbalance
and speaks volumes of the under provision of resources faced by
this age-group in earlier years.

To some extent, the 80% figure is a pointless statistic. After
all, everybody knows that it is no reflection on the abilities of
older people. But educators must not under-estimate the effect
that older learners' own knowledge of their unqualified status has
had on their confidence and self-esteem over the years. This is
a theme to which we will return later.

A second major characteristic of this group is that they are,
paradoxically, younger and fitter either than they have ever been
before or than the rest of us now recognise. Better health care
and ameliorated housing conditions have clearly helped in bringing
this about but a later phenomenon has had an even greater effect.
Early retirement is now much more widespread than ever could
have been predicted even five years ago. Most local authorities
and many companies now have schemes to enable people to retire
at 55, or even earlier, on enhanced pensions and/or with lump
sums to cushion the effect.

More than ever, therefore, do educators need to lose their
ageist ideas about what kind of thing older learners need or would
like. The anodyne and often patronising activities of the 'Darby
and Joan' or the 'Silver Threads' clubs seem less and less likely
to appeal to a generation attuned to packaged holidays on the

continent and all that they entail. Anyone who has been brushed aside by the crowds of pensioners massing at the Saga holidays point on Victoria Station or fought for a seat on British Rail during their November special offers for pensioners will appreciate the point.

Finally, there are simply more of them. From 1971, when there were twice as many youngsters in school than there were retired people, to 1981 when the numbers equalled out, there has been in Brian Groombridge's phrase, 'a demographic transformation' which will see, by the end of this decade, twice as many people in retirement as there will be pupils in schools - a neat about-turn in less than 20 years. Perhaps pressures in the polling booths by then will encourage politicians to make a parallel switch in the funding required to meet the educational needs of the two groups - and will the education service be ready for that - or even a watered-down version of it?

If we have to re-think our ideas about who the new breed of older learners are, we must also, obviously, think again about what we mean by education and recogise that courses, tutors and classes are but one manifestation of the learning process. Above all, we need to re-affirm the concept of recurrent education - the meeting of changing needs throughout life, rather than what Eric Midwinter has called the current 'apprentice-bound' education system.

ii. What is the Community Education Approach?

Community educators are a relatively new breed of people in the education service. Some would say they have their tutorial roots in the Mechanics' Institutes early in the century or, more likely still, the Village Colleges of Henry Morris's Cambridgeshire in the thirties. Their outreach roots are less tangible but might be traced through the early health visitors to the informal adult education approaches of the Education Priority Area movement in the late sixties and early seventies. At their current stage of evolution they are still most likely to be found in educational institutions, albeit of the more open kind, - in community primary schools, adult education centres and community colleges.

Increasingly though, they are found in other less formal community settings - taking education to the people rather than waiting for customers to come through the door. Largely trained as professionals, usually teachers, community educators pride themselves on their particular professional skills, different from either community workers or adult educators but owing something to both. They have open discussions with members of the community about educational needs rather than taking all the decisions themselves, - they start where people are 'at'.

They seek to meet those needs in new ways, breaking down old barriers, creatively using existing resources - human and environmental - rather than forever seeking new ones. They are concerned with the process of learning and not just the content of it - eschewing the expert-client approach for a collaborative, self-mobilising and ultimately autonomous one.

Much of it is about confidence-building. If we lay before the community an à la carte menu of educational dishes and they fail to water at the mouth, are we to bemoan their lack of good taste or, equally pointlessly, sack the cook and bring in a new one? Might we, instead, ask the customers to devise the menu, enlist their aid in the cooking and, not least, in the serving? Of course, not to carry the metaphor too far, we would meet the resistance of the community who would soon explain that they were not trained or qualified to do any of this. Confidence is noticeably lacking, in educational terms, in the vast majority of potential participants, particularly in the older age range, who for so long have been denied the opportunity to join in.

Confidence does not come, of course, merely from the availability of a new 'product'. It has to be painstakingly built by skilled workers using the tools of sensitivity, listening skills and respect rather than the traditional pedagogic skills of knowledge transmission. It is often a slow process; it has setbacks and disappointments and needs stamina and perserverance as much as imagination and creativity. Without it, though, we might as well confine ourselves to laying on a ready-made programme on a take-it-or-leave-it basis, and cease concerning ourselves with the failures such approaches have had in reaching the bulk of the population.

Some of the work done in community education 'outreach' activities, particularly in disadvantaged areas, and perhaps above all with the frequently isolated and economically-depressed younger women who tend to be the solitary adult in one-parent families, has shown the way forward. A recently completed project supported by the Bernard Van Leer Foundation, and using the community education services of Coventry, Liverpool, Birmingham and the West Isles of Scotland, is a good example. This Open University project aimed to use enlightened and clearly-written materials about child-rearing practices which would be accessible to groups not traditionally familiar with OU programmes; essentially, the workers in these very disparate locations had to devise new methods of reaching out to such groups. Significantly, the relative-recently devised methods of local community educators seemed to prove the most effective means of bringing groups together.

Such methods included slotting this project into the contexts
of outgoing community education groups where professionals had
already established relationships with local residents, or knew
how to go about it. Seeking to reach the most disadvantaged people
in difficult rural terrain on the one hand, and somewhat notorious
urban neighbourhoods on the other, they gradually raised the
confidence of large numbers of participants. This was despite
their finding all too frequently an almost numbing apathy, border-
ing on total withdrawal from community life in the more extreme
cases.

One colleague describes her work in the early stages of
reaching such groups as <u>double-digging</u> - the careful preparation
of the ground before attempting to plant new seeds. She means
by this the whole range of community education outreach methods -
knocking on doors to talk face-to-face with people; the gradual
building of groups of two or three in homes before ever attempting
to integrate people into larger groups; concentration on needs
identified by the people themselves rather than the purveying of
a pre-determined set of ideas or materials. All of this, of course,
needs to be carried out with non-judgemental attitudes to the
value - systems of others and a preparedness to become involved
in the issues facing the residents in their own communities.

Sheila Karran, who was the community education worker in
Coventry for the Open University project, learned these skills in
her previous position as an Education Visitor in the city - itself
a position which was first created in an earlier community
education experiment, the Educational Priority Area Project.
Since then, Sheila Karran has continued the development of these
ideas in her current work as a home-school organiser for the
city's Community Education Project. Sheila Karran's concentration is invariably on the development of peer-group support
based on the certain knowledge that ordinary people can be
encouraged to support each other in the group situation and that
the role of the sensitive professional is that of an enabler and
facilitator - breaking away from paternalism and striving for a
collaborative and colleaginal relationship. In no way is this an
abdication of professionalism. On the contrary, it requires a
more enlightened, more demanding and ultimately enhanced role
for the professional.

In 1978, Flo Robinson, an ex-head of an infants' school who
was by then a community education worker in a disadvantaged area
of the north of Coventry, was determined to involve a group of
mothers in the teaching of reading to their children. Almost to
her own surprise, she found herself up to her neck in discussions
about unpaid gas bills, marital problems, rent arrears, welfare

benefits, condensation problems and a whole series of other issues which to 'her mums' seemed even more pressing than the achievements of their youngsters in the classroom. So was the concept of 'double-digging' born in Flo Robinson's mind - not as an intellectual, theoretical concept but as a glaring practical demand born of necessity. Her later success in achieving her more limited original aims on the reading front could, she believes, be attributed at least as much to the mutual support those women gained in sharing feelings and insights about other issues as to their more structured discussions about reading schemes and the like. Certainly, observers reported great difficulty in discerning the main purpose of these group meetings yet all commented glowingly on the relaxed and informal atmosphere and the obvious value of the group to the women concerned.

Another project, originated by the Community Education Development Centre in Hounslow and Coventry owes much to the pioneering work of the Education Visitors mentioned earlier. Called H. E. L. P. - Home-based Early Learning Project - it borrows unashamedly from the commercial world of party-plan selling to take education into the homes of people in several neighbourhoods. Just as Education Visitors brought parents together to discuss the wider issues of education as well as their own child's progress in school, the HELP workers organise informal get-togethers in the homes of residents. Here they are led by local people, 'trained' beforehand by professionals and carrying a stock of some low-cost materials, games, but above all, educational ideas. Their successes have exploded many educational myths, but, most importantly, they have highlighted a new and valuable method of outreach work, easily replicated and costing little.

iii. Who Might Do This Kind of Work?

If most of the strategies described here have been aimed at people with young families, can any of them be translated into effective tools for working with older learners? There seems to be an overwhelming argument that they can.

Paradoxically, the fact that more than one quarter of retired people live alone, and the even more chilling statistic that one fifth of them are in receipt of supplementary benefit, provide part of the proof. First, retired people living alone are clearly in need of the kind of contact which some of these strategies have so clearly provided to other, equally isolated people. Arguably, old people alone are even more vulnerable than the lone mother of a young child who at least has her raison d'être tugging at her skirt to remind her all to palpably of her role. Second, sheer

economic necessity prevents all too many older people from
taking advantage of the too-few learning opportunities which are
presented to them. Even the LEA fees are prohibitive in some
areas of the country.

An even more telling argument is the much more positive one
that this age-group of people seems more than any other, except
the very young, to be ready to join a group. Of all the myths
about older people, the most cruel, yet most easily disproved, is
the one which says that they prefer to be alone. Almost all groups
which begin with a view to attracting this age-group seem to
prosper. Indeed the surprising thing is how ready older people
are to join groups which offer little more than the mere opportunity to mix with others. It is as if the whole community
education approach has been designed with this age-group in mind.

If any of these strategies for work with older people are to
work, conventional attitudes are going to have to change. It simply
will not do to expect the retired to sit quietly looking at their
retirement clock until it is too late to experience again the joy of
learning. We must now look at the positive side of retirement -
recognising that here are the wisest and most experienced people
in society. Then we can reasonably ask them what new contribution they intend to make to the community, for surely the
community cannot afford to lose their skills. Once this new
psychology takes hold, we have the right climate to enable people
to learn, to lead, to take control of their own lives.

Fortunately, there are already some startling examples of
success which are capable of replication elsewhere. Vera
Southgate, in Stoke-on-Trent, working for the Beth Johnson
Foundation, found it almost impossible to persuade the local
leisure committee that the elderly should have their own special
time in the council's swimming pools. When she was finally
granted an hour, it was at the inauspicious time of eight o'clock
on Friday evenings. To everyone's astonishment, a minimum of
publicity produced a massive response from older people. Really,
the only surprise is that we are surprised.

Birmingham's FIRCONE scheme - Friends in Retirement - is
a fine example of the community education notion of using the most
readily able resource in the community - other people, to provide
a wide range of study opportunities for others. Groups are led by
facilitators who are usually retired themselves.

The Community Education Development Centre's 'Senior
Action' project in Stoke-on-Trent and Northampton aims to find
opportunities for retired people to make a new contribution to their
communities using whatever skills they have learned from their
previous jobs or gained in other ways during their lives. Like any

scheme which genuinely seeks to involve people, it is run by
retired people themselves - the first set of skills required is the
ability to run the project.

iv. Who Can Carry It Out?

Eric Midwinter has argued for a 'barefoot teacher' approach
towards working with older learners - a home-visiting tutor,
perhaps a paraprofessional - visiting homes on a weekly basis.
All community educators will recognise the style. And there can
be little doubt that this precisely matches the unorthodox out-
reaching methods described earlier. It is, of course, only one
approach and since many are going to be needed, it may be useful
to look at the 'breeds' of people required.

Clearly, no government in the foreseeable future is likely to
sanction the creation of a new breed of professionals to facilitate
the learning structures of older students. It may also be true
that this would not be the best solution in any case. Much more
likely, and perhaps more desirable, is the recruitment of new
cadres of volunteers - along the lines of FIRCONE and Senior
Action - who will adopt the community education approach and
become enablers in their own right, rather than surrogate
professionals providing a watered-down tutorial service.

If this were to be done on any ambitious scale - indeed if it
were to be done at all - it would need professional support.
Volunteers need training, initial and in-service, so to speak, and
ongoing support in the field. They need the kind of informed
backing offered to residents in the HELP scheme, or that
provided by Sheila Karran to her mothers' groups. It needs, then,
a re-cycling of existing professionals to act in this way and to
spread their influence widely through training the trainers for
group work.

Whenever this kind of networking operation is mounted, there
sooner or later arises the need for paraprofessionals - and these
may be nearer to the 'barefoot teachers' Eric Midwinter had in
mind. They are likely to be the more successful of the volunteers
since volunteering invariably throws up those with real talent in
any particular field. They will be the most assiduous trainers,
the best empathisers, the most effective communicators. More
likely than not, they will work part-time and they will provide not
only a cost-effective force but one less likely to be concerned
with its own vested interests.

None of this can be done for nothing. For too long, community
educators have managed the 'bricks-without-straw' departments
of local authorities. Cost-effective does not mean cost-free.
Re-cycled professionals will be capable of training the volunteers
and the paraprofessionals who will be the cadre-leaders. But

all the work generated will need financial support for payment of paraprofessionals, for expenses of volunteers, for materials and equipment to carry out the work. Nevertheless, the greatest need will remain the changed attitude by local authorities to provide the professional scheme leaders and by those professionals who will be required to exchange their former roles for the new one of trainer of the trainers, network organiser, innovator, motivator and inter-professional linkman.

Where can it all take place? In the best spirit of community education, the community's own resources will be used. So the pubs and clubs will be as likely as the schools and colleges to house the groups of learners. Tutors will venture into homes - HELP-style - on an informal group-work basis and on only a one-to-one basis where people are incapacitated. Others will operate with groups where people are in residential care - and even in this precedents already exist. In other words, wherever people with needs are, there will the tutors need to go.

It seems strange that the process of education is so bound up in our minds with schools. Odder still that we continue to accept the Victorian notion that schooling is for the young in society - all very well given the Victorians' narrow concept of education but ludicrous given today's broadly accepted notion of lifelong learning. But such a notion becomes an empty promise if it is not applied to people who may not uncommonly spend nearly as long in retirement as they have done in their working lives.

In arguments about unemployment and the costs of factory closures, for example, it has become fashionable to think of a 'social audit' - taking account of the social costs of closure as well as the immediate removal of the factory-owners' losses. Perhaps it is timely, therefore, to take a social audit of the concept of retirement and of not making available the community education resources to make a contribution to the education of the third age. We may then take an Elizabethan decision to abandon yet another (and provenly dangerous) invention of the Victorians, - retirement - and replace it with a new 'Third Age Learning Stage'. Community educators have the tools all ready to make it happen.

(B) The Mutual Aid/Self-Help Movement   Michael Young
Self-help and mutual aid are flourishing not because of the present
government but despite it.   Since 1979 there has been a sad
running down of the welfare state which was built up so painstakingly in the previous half century.   There have been cuts and
half-cuts and the threats of cuts, and perhaps just as significant
as that in its effects has been the deliberate spreading of
discouragement.   To judge by the way some ministers have
talked, and are talking, there is something almost reprehensible
about being in the public service at all (except for the forces and
the police).   In the past, it was considered a sign of civilisation
that people could work in jobs where they were not motivated by
profit but by concern to perform a public service not driven by
commercial dictates.   The people whose mission seems to be to
undermine morale amongst the millions engaged in education,
health, social services and public housing have undoubtedly had
some success.   All their talk about the paramount need (as they
see it) to reduce public spending has been enfeebling.   Millions
of the best, most useful and most public spirited people in the
country are threatened with the status of drone, of being a
'burden' on the rest of us, when the fact is that without them the
rest of us would be in real poverty, material and spiritual.
Dismantle morale in the public services and where would the rest
of us be?

As if to add insult to injury, these same ministers are inclined
to give self-help a bad name as well, by suggesting it as an alternative to the public services - cut down, they say, on the one and
compensate by a growth of the other.   This is only mischief.
Self-help can never be a substitute for collective organisation,
informal mutual aid a substitute for formal mutual aid through
the means of the welfare state.   The U3A could never, and should
never, take the place of ordinary universities or adult education;
self-help groups like the Spastics Society or the Schizophrenia
Fellowship never take the place of the NHS; housing associations
take the place of local authorities.   The formal social services
need the support of informal, led by the family itself; likewise
the informal or voluntary self-help movements need the backing
of the welfare state.   It is no use just sharing out time, care and
money within the little domain of Puddlecombe or Perth.   There
needs also to be a grand sharing between all the citizens of the
nation if their individual rights are to be respected wherever they
live and whatever they do.   There needs also to be a willingness
to back self-help groups with public funds wherever they are
essential to support an initiative which would otherwise wither.

The best hope is that, once this present period of penny-pinching is over, welfare state and welfare self-help will flourish together, in partnership. There are many good examples already to point the way forward, like housing associations which combine state funds and voluntary effort, or local enterprise trusts like the one at St Helens or the many voluntary bodies which look after handicapped children. Many of the most flourishing mutual aid groups are supported by public funds. Long may it be so. That is one way forward for the welfare state which has added something of crucial value to the original Beveridge conception. But the promise will be blighted unless the main structure in education, health, social services and the rest is kept in being and, more then that, nourished.

I think that needs to be said in order to dissociate myself from any misguided person who sees the U3A or any other self-help body as something which is going to do the government's work. But that having been said, I can now without compunction declare my belief in the value of self-help as a supplement to the welfare state. Perhaps I can best make my point by an illustration drawn from my own experience.

Marianne Rigge and I had worked at the National Consumer Council for some years when we decided that the 'consumer movement' needed a mutual aid wing to it. The path had been beaten for us by Eric Midwinter who had promoted bulk buy groups as a modern form of the original consumer co-operative, more like the Rochdale Equitable Society than the Co-operative Wholesale Society. But more remained to be done and some of it could perhaps be fostered by the Mutual Aid Centre which we founded.

No new initiative that I've heard of has gone smoothly and the Mutual Aid Centre has been no exception. We have had our crop of mistakes and failures, like the attempt we made to save the London Co-operative Society by supporting reform candidates for the last democratic election held before the LCS was taken over by the national body, Co-operative Retail Services. We were probably twenty years too late and our manifesto, Mutual Aid in a Selfish Society, addressed to our fellow-members of the London Society, did not bring out many votes. In general, apathy reigned. Arteries had hardened.

So we turned instead to the small and the new, while still aiming to do what the co-operative societies had done at their best, that is become self-supporting through providing a service that members wanted and were prepared to pay for as well as work for. I had many years before, when I started Which? magazine, seen the Consumers' Association in that light, as a self-help body which was in the nature of an information co-

operative. Members paid their subscriptions for an information
service which they all benefited from and increasingly, also,
they shared information direct by telling each other through the
medium of the Association what their own experience had been
with their various makes of car, washing machines or General
Practitioners. The same idea should be capable of translation
to other fields.

The first big effort went into a motorists' co-operative. We
learnt a lot from Sweden. It has 800 service stations specialising
in DIY, with bays specially equipped for the poorer motorist who
does his or her own servicing and repair and with expert advice
on tap to support the members who help each other. Our first
station took a long time to negotiate because we had no capital
and had to stitch together some £$\frac{1}{4}$ million to pay for the building
and equip it to a high standard. The site we chose was at Milton
Keynes and the name of our place the same as in Sweden, OK, so
that we are known there as MKOK.

The station sells to its members and outsiders petrol, oil,
accessories, everything that the most modern garage has on
offer. In principle you can get everything there that, as a
motorist, you need, and maybe a few things that you don't. But
in all departments except DIY the competition is fierce, much
more so than anything the Consumers' Association has to face.
Even so, it has worked and in 1984 a second, larger (but still
small) station is to open in Brixton in London which will improve
on model one in respect of everything we've learnt at Milton
Keynes. With any luck and a great deal of hard work there
should be a national chain of these motorists co-operatives by
1990. We shall see.

The next endeavour has been in a quite different field again,
the recycling of domestic appliances and furniture. Despite the
economic depression modern Britain is a throw-away society,
wasting precious materials and energy on a colossal scale, much
of it disposed of on dumps of one kind and another. It should be
possible to save more and waste less. With so much unemployment an attempt should (it seemed to us) be made to recycle
such products and simultaneously to train young people as service
men and craftsmen. The first co-operative workshop called
Brass Tacks was started, with help from the Manpower Services
Commission, in Hackney, the second in Lambeth, the third in
Greenwich, and they have spread out around the country from
there. Most are dependent for wages on the MSC. One in
Southwark is not, and has to make ends meet on its own.

These have led to the latest venture, the College of Health
and its journal Self-Health, which is perhaps more like the

Consumers Association than it is like OK or Brass Tacks. The inspiration was given by the self-help groups which have flourished so exceedingly for people with disabilities or common problems to do with their health or that of their relatives. We have on our computer the names of 1200 of them, varying from large national bodies with a far-flung network of branches like the Spastics Society, the Multiple Sclerosis Society or the Diabetics Society to small but vigorous bodies like In Touch or the Dystonia Society. They are usually started by a sufferer or a small group of sufferers meeting in a private home. This is followed by a letter to a newspaper or a talk on the radio which heralds the beginning of a mass membership. The largest and richest support research on a grand scale and inform and influence the medical professions too. But almost always the foundation is the small cells of people who meet regularly and support each other on a continuing basis. At the centre is an information and co-ordinating centre while out in the cities, towns and villages are the small groups of people meeting each other face to face where the real work is done.

The new College of Health, as a self-help body not specialised like so many of the other 1200, met with a ready response. 1,000 people joined in the first month after it was launched. The information the College will collect and distribute is to serve the four main purposes, as I set them out in the first issue of Self-Health, in terms of prevention, self-care, treatment and alternative medicine.

With my own interest in self-help, whether expressed through the College of Health or in other ways, it was perhaps natural that I should be excited by the University of the Third Age. My own particular contribution to it has been the Third Age Project in Devon. This is a mutual support body for unemployed and early retired people over 40 as well as for people who have retired. The mix seems to work well. More and more local projects are being formed in the towns of Devon, as chapter nine describes.

I am glad there is such variety within the U3A. Every local initiative is unique. There needs to be the maximum local autonomy but backed up by a small national organisation which fosters an information co-operative for every locality. That is the way it is going and it seems as right for the U3A as it does for the College of Health or any other flourishing self-help group that I know.

PART 2.   THE PARTICULAR : CASE-STUDIES OF BRITISH U3As.

Chapter 7

THE UNIVERSITY OF THE THIRD AGE - NATIONWIDE

DIANNE NORTON

It is extraordinary how coherent a pattern emerges, given
the superficially differing vantage-points of the observers:
the moral urgency of Peter Laslett's splendid declaration
of the rights of older people to education; Michel Philibert's
elegant exposition of the historic necessity of such a
phenomenon; the alignment of Paula Allman's penetrating
analysis of the adult learning process with the self-help
approach; David Radcliffe's demonstration of the movements'
worldwide validity; and the apposite and empathetic character
of community education and mutual aid, as so lucidly
expressed by John Rennie and Michael Young.
What has throughout been taken for granted, but what is
central to the reflections of all the essayists, indeed
passionately embraced by them, is the independent status
of elderly people. Above all, and from all those standpoints,
the message is clear and direct, and it is one now constantly
pressed by all whose task it is to formulate social policy
for the elderly. It concerns the elderly person as actor,
rather than spectator, as doer and participant, not as passive
recipient, as a liberated and autonomous personality, and
never a manipulated cypher.
The running theme, then, has been self-determination, and
the overall objective that of older people mobilising their
own energies and controlling their own educational future.
It remains to be seen whether there are, so to speak,
buttered parsnips as well as fine words, and, in this the
second part of the book, we turn to the day-by-day detail
of four real-life U3As, prefaced by a description of the
current incidence of U3A groups in Britain and their present
stages of development. This has been prepared by, and the
four case-studies drawn together by Dianne Norton.
Dianne Norton studied, taught and researched in the social
sciences both in her native Canada and in London. In 1981
she became the Co-ordinator of the Forum on the Rights of

Elderly People to Education (F. R. E. E.), the information
exchange and pressure group promoting the general thesis
that older citizens should have an improved educational
deal.   In the same year Dianne Norton was appointed
Executive Secretary to the National Committee of the
University of the Third Age.   As such she has been largely
responsible for the successful administration of British
U3As in their formative years and she is uniquely placed
to survey the national scene.

The University of the Third Age in Britain has been launched
more times than a rubber boat in a high wind.   That is not to say
that any of these starts were in any way 'false starts'or that the
lightweight craft was bounced backwards by a hostile public.   The
handful of people initially involved in U3A were, from the outset,
excited by its prospects but assumptions that the nation's press
would be equally enthusiastic were ill-founded.   On the 17th of
June, 1981, a press release announced the launch of the first
University of the Third Age Committee, in Cambridge.
'The Committee of the proposed University of the Third Age
in Cambridge held its first meeting at Trinity College last
week.   The University of the Third Age in Cambridge would
be the first educational institution in this country run entirely
by and for elderly and retired people.   The Committee intends
to draw up a plan to be presented at a Public Meeting in the
Guildhall, Cambridge, at 7:30 p.m. on Monday, July, 20th.
It is hoped that at this meeting citizens of the Cambridge area
will declare their wish to be involved in this exciting new
educational initiative. '
Although this historic document fell on deaf journalistic ears,
the meeting itself was deemed by all who attended   to be a great
success.   After introductions by Peter Laslett of Trinity College,
Cambridge who was the first person to see the practical possibi-
lities of the Third Age idea in this country, and Eric Midwinter,
the keynote address was given by specially invited guest,
Professeur Michel Philibert from the Université du Troisième
Age in Grenoble.   Michel Philibert has long association with the
French movement and spoke as inspiringly of its value as he
writes about it in chapter three.
But the implications of this meeting went far beyond the launch
of the local initiative.   Eric Midwinter reported the gathering on
BBC'S Radio 4 'You and Yours' programme and sparked off nearly
four hundred letters from all over the country.
'I write to record my interest.   Your broadcast leads me to believe
that you are suggesting something that I long thought must one day

develop, making learning accessible to those who realise its
value for its own sake'......... and 'I have been trying to teach
myself something of the Arts and although I find it stimulating to
study, I know it would be beneficial to have some guidance and an
opportunity to communicate with like-minded people. I am 72
years old and live alone.'...... or 'I am quite convinced that
such an establishment would discover a lot of talent otherwise
going completely to waste.' 'I am 68 years old and live in a
dreamy Dorset town,' wrote another. 'The usual outlets are not
available here, firstly, transport is almost non-existent. The
WEA caters for people who have finished their education, namely
retired professionals. They want flora and fauna and architecture and get it. I once enrolled in a class for beginners learning
to type but it was for young people hoping to earn a living. I
would like to learn the basics of English, how to compose and
write a letter properly. In fact I would like to start where I left
off compulsory schooling at 11 years old. I passed the scholarship exam to go to grammar school but developed rheumatic
fever and never went to school again. My dearest possession is
a letter from my head teacher telling me I passed the exam. I
always wanted to be a teacher, bit late now, but I've never lost
my desire for learning'...... and so they rolled in.

It was these letters, rather than the press reaction, which we
felt indicated the true level of interest in the idea and since that
time, every public mention, no matter how small, has brought
an encouraging and widespread response from old, lonely and
bored people, from people about to retire and worried at the
prospect, from people already heavily involved in voluntary
activities but intrigued by this one, by relatives of elderly people
concerned about their lack of involvement and from people with
professional interests.

Peter Laslett undertook to draw up the 'Objects, Principles
and Institutional Forms of the University of the Third Age in
Cambridge' and it is this document, completed in August 1981
which has become the basis for all subsequent philosophical and
policy statements made by what is now the National Committee.
But, in order to respond to that first tide of letters, we composed
a statement outlining the meaning of 'Third Age', briefly
mentioning its development in France and suggesting the sorts of
activities which might possibly be developed in this country. We
also included one concept which had in fact been central to all the
early discussions, but which has subsequently been modified, or
laid aside completely in some cases. The relevant paragraph is;
    'The key word to understanding how such a University of the
    Third age might actually work in 'negotiation'. The ultimate

structure, we believe, should be a self-generated governing
body of elderly and retired people, whose primary task
would be to negotiate for the use of whatever facilities and
resources, including teachers, where necessary to the
development of whatever educational activities they chose
to pursue.'

The concept of the Third Age Committee as a 'negotiator' owes
its origin to the existing style of the French movement and to
Peter Laslett's conviction, following a study tour abroad,
(described in chapter two) that the educational institutions of
this country must be forced, if necessary, to open their doors
on a grand scale, to elderly learners. At the present time this
function of negotiator has not been realised in any extensive
sense. Certainly, as we will see, as we look at the development
of local groups where negotiation has been used, it has been on
a limited scale for the use of rooms, or for publicity. The U3A
in London is the only one to have taken this further and is actually
negotiating with a variety of providers of educational opportunities, usually short courses, for access for limited numbers of
their members.

In half a dozen areas university departments, schools and
colleges are playing an initiative role, but the impetus has come
from the professional staff and not from would be third age users,
as originally envisaged. Peter Laslett's Objects and Principles
are, however, heavily embued with the philosophy of self-help,
which was one factor in the change of emphasis. Ironically,
another contributing factor has probably been the success of the
Cambridge movement in doing everything for themselves. Right
from the outset the enthusiasts they gathered to them were
sufficiently talented, experienced and imaginative to proceed
from theory to practice without recourse to outside advice. If,
as they have now decided, their organisation has become too
large and too complex to be run entirely on a voluntary basis,
then they themselves will have to fund administrative help but
will continue to make their own decisions on all U3A matters.
Obviously Cambridge is an area oozing with scholastic and
cultural advantages and many of the U3A members are in some
way 'touched' by the academic world. But Cambridge is our
'prototype' and much has been learned from their experience.
However, it is necessary and advantageous to study the progress
and requirements of quite different environments. They may
find that they need to be negotiators. Although negotiations may
open some academic doors, a real break through will, I believe,
occur in a more indirect way. The spread of Third Age groups
will eventually create a climate of opinion in which educational

pursuits are accepted as being appropriate activities for older adults and in which demands can rightfully be made on traditional providers.

The longtitudinal development of the University of the Third Age in Britain can be illustrated by taking a latitudinal look at it now. A cross-section reveals local groups in various stages of development, manifesting similar enough features to form an enlightening pattern.

(A) Stage One: The Spontaneous Initiative

Perhaps in the future the National U 3A Committee will have sufficient resources to employ or at least provide expenses for a peripatetic organiser who would be able to move in on fertile ground and promote new developments. However, in the past and for the present, we rely entirely on one or more people in an area giving the incentive, committing their time and energy and doing what they can to bring local groups into being. From that very first batch of letters, following Eric Midwinter's broadcast, one or two correspondents have now become committed organisers. Several others came as 'students' to the experimental Easter School held in Cambridge in March 1982 and left determined to start groups of their own. Others have read about the movement's progress and written asking what they can do and some 'beginners' are professional adult educators either fully employed or partially retired who, through their experiences with older learners, have grasped the possibilities of U 3A.

In September 1982 the National Committee, which had grown out of the original Cambridge Committee and was now chaired by Michael Young, staged another launch. This time it was to announce the publication of U3A DIY: A practical manual designed to guide groups and individuals wishing to start a Third Age University or similar self-help educational project. U3A DIY has been successful enough to be updated and reprinted. It contains an introductory section on WHAT is a University of the Third Age. The HOW section gives a step-by-step path, from commitment to realisation, for the new organiser to follow. It also includes sample letters, a poster, questionnaire, record sheet, suggested themes for study groups, an item on doing your own research and a media page, as well as short case studies of some differing U3A groups already underway. The final section tells people WHERE to go for help, resources, information and the location of all existing groups. The pack contains catalogues and hand-outs from a variety of organisations, such as the National Extension College, Help the Aged and Age

Concern publications departments and radio and TV companies.
Many new organisers have made use of these materials when
planning their first moves.

The other service which the National office offers at this
stage is a list of names and addresses of people who have made
enquiries about U3A from their particular area. All letters
from places where currently no contact or group exists are
indexed so that, when someone does take the initiative of bringing
together like-minded people, there is a nucleus of informed
people as a starting point. Experience seems to show that it is
best to start with small gatherings of interested people. As U3A
DIY says, 'It has been found that explaining U3A is an extremely
personal business. It is a new notion and it is not susceptible to
explanation in a few key words in a poster.' In some cases these
initial groups have been made up entirely of retired people; in
other areas they have been professional educators and, in still
others, it has been a combination of the two that has got things
going. They have all seemed to share the need, whatever their
backgrounds, for an intense discussion of the underlying philosophy, the possible forms and the nomenclature of the new idea.
As Eric Midwinter reminds in chapter one, the labels associated
with old people and words such as 'university' are heavy with
connotations which bring out strong feelings in most people, so
a considerable amount of time has been spent in early meetings
in trying to find some compromise or an acceptable and catch
title. To date we have a clutch of Universities, as well as the
Third Age Learning Circle/Conference/College(TALC), the Third
Age Project (TAP), Self-help Activities in Retirement (SHARE),
The Leicester Education and Research Network (LEARN), The
Association of Students of the Third Age (ASTA) and the Yeovil
Shared Interest Society (YSIS), as well as a group in Stevenage
who dislike both university and third age and have chosen the
title 'Leisure 50'.

The particular demography of each locale, the existence of
adult education provision and facilities, such as meeting rooms,
are taken into consideration at these early meetings. The
situation in Norfolk, for instance, where a would-be-organiser
is finding little enthusiasm in Norwich, which is basically well-
catered for, but a different response in the scattered pockets of
rural population, presents two quite different pictures. This
first stage of development is a tricky one. It requires the
commitment of time and energy and frequently of money. Many
of these early organisers who have set out to float the idea with
no help from institutions or other bodies have used their own
money for photocopying, postage and phone calls. In some cases

the U3A National Committee has been able to help with a very
modest grant. In those areas where the initiative has been taken
by persons with 'institutional connections', help with publicity and
communications and the provision of meeting places has generally
been 'absorbed', in many cases, in departmental expenses.

(B) Stage Two: The Public Gathering
In most cases, the originating Committee has organised a public
meeting or one-day conference to launch the local initiative on
the public scene. Local radio and press have usually been
helpful in publicising such meetings as have the libraries. Some
meetings are open to the general public while some only to the
invited who may be those people who had responded to various
items of publicity and written in asking for more information, or,
as in the case of the initial meeting at Surrey University, they
may be mostly representatives of various professional bodies and
departments concerned either with the elderly in the community
or adult education provision. It has been found to be important
to invite representation from as many interested groups as
possible, if for no other reason than to allay any suspicions that
may arise about the future intentions of U3A. In some areas
where people from, for instance, the LEA and WEA and the
university extension department have not been included in early
discussions or kept informed, they have reacted defensively when
faced with what looks like a possible threat to their student
numbers. In the few areas where difficulties have arisen they
have generally been resolved through consultation and general
agreement to co-operate. In Lancaster, for example, the U3A
has agreed that, if a circumstance arises where any of its groups
wishes to move into a more structured or 'taught' pattern of
activities, it might become a WEA class. Alternatively, any
WEA class which becomes too small to be viable could transform
itself into a U3A self-help group. In Surrey, where the area to
be served is large and the population scattered, it is hoped that
early consultation will ensure the possibilities of using the
established network of adult education centres as a basis for U3A
groups throughout the county.

(C) Stage Three: The Working Party
From the stage of the public meeting the pattern most commonly
followed has been the setting up of a small working party..... a
group of dedicated people who will look more intensely at the best
ways of translating theory into practice given the particular
circumstances of the area. A lot of effort is put in at this stage
to finding out what resources, human and otherwise, are

available in the area. Organisers have been known to go out and actually stop people in the streets and ask what they thought of the U3A idea. In Hyde, Cheshire, members of a group from the Community School, in the course of a summer project which involved knocking on doors, included questions designed to locate people interested in the Third Age idea. Other groups have used questionnaires based on the sample provided in U3A DIY to elicit details such as previous occupation, interests, what new interests people wanted to develop, what people felt they could contribute (accommodation/transport/administrative skills/teaching), how much time they were prepared to devote per week, how much they would be willing to pay, information about housebound people and so on. Having located the potential resources, the working party must then devise the best ways of using what is available to meet the wishes of prospective members.

The Association of Students of the Third Age (ASTA) in Oxford has developed an interesting variation on this theme. They have made themselves available on one day a week in a public and central location and advertised the fact that members of ASTA would be there to advice older adults on educational matters in general. They discuss with enquirers what sort of educational experience they are looking for and will point people in the direction of courses or services on offer from the Open University, the LEA, WEA, Extra-mural department etc. They will also register any interests that are not catered for through existing provision and hope to be able to fill these gaps through their own organisation

It is not all plain sailing. Take U3A in Mid-Wales: despite a £1000 grant from the Manpower Services Commission 'Opportunities for Volunteering in Wales' scheme, Roger Palmer, the organiser, found it difficult to gather together a committee, based on Montgomery, from over a wide area. A postal shot to interested parties and five hundred excellent posters -'This Life is the Great Schoolmaster.......Experience the Mighty Volume' - throughout Powys proved equally unsuccessful. Roger Palmer now favours a much more locally based project, perhaps in Newtown, with less of an academic bent. He is convinced the need exists and hopes, perhaps through a project focus (such as a look at rural transport for the elderly or local attitudes to ageism) to further the cause.

(D) Stage Four: The Mainstream Programme
In order to set up a variety of study groups, each looking at particular subjects, it is necessary to have a reasonable number of members which is not always the case in the early stages.

What has happened in Stevenage, Harpenden, and Nottingham is that the U3A group, which may consist of around 25 people, has started out by planning a programme of regular weekly or fortnightly meetings. Members are asked to make presentations on topics in which they have some interest and experience and to lead discussions, or in some cases, speakers are invited in who are non-members and.the discussion prolonged over two sessions. In Stevenage the general meetings have now also given birth to two or three smaller study groups studying languages and other topics.

The areas where organisation has been successful and swift have tended to be fairly homogeneously populated and relatively concentrated. Transport here is not, on the whole, a problem. It is easy to spark off an interest in locally based activities. But other areas have more hurdles to overcome before they can really commence operations. Oddly enough, some rural and urban areas are faced with very similar problems. In Manchester and Sussex initial meetings have indicated a good degree of interest. Manchester held an introductory meeting to which they invited interested professionals from a wide range of organisations and educational institutions, as well as retired people who had expressed an interest. Leslie Jones, from the staff of the University department of Adult and Continuing Education was asked to co-ordinate efforts to launch U3A in Manchester. The ad hoc committee hoped to arouse enough support to start a programme of activities and had previously manned a stall at the Manchester College of Adult Education during enrolment week and distributed questionnaires to retired people who came in. However, despite much planning and enthusiasm, activities in Manchester have, to date, been disappointing. They have found that the greatest problem is the spread of the population, the distances and the paucity of numbers actually involved. They did manage to get two groups together in different areas, one looking at local history and the other at computers, but the question of how to provide leadership in a variety of subjects over a large area in which travel is both difficult and expensive, remains unanswered. As with Mid-Wales, the likely solution does seem to be the development of purely local groups, wherever a spark appears, and then, eventually, the spread of enough groups to create a support network covering the whole conurbation. It is interesting that, in some degree, the problem of the diverse rural area and the sprawling conurbation turn out to be much the same, and a specifically localised approach seems to be the answer.

In Sussex and also in Gloucestershire the problems proved

insurmountable to volunteer organisers. However, while the
latter county's local contact gave up the struggle and the Sussex
U3A failed in its first attempt for other reasons, a new initiative
there looks much more solid. Peter Grainge of Bishop Otter
College of Further Education in Chichester briefed a number of
his colleagues concerned with extension work and adult education,
as well as a representative of the LEA, on U3A. He then called
a small meeting for intense discussion of the issues. The
professionals felt that a U3A network would be an extension of the
college's services to the community and that the college could
benefit from the feedback from more mature students and that
some may be reintroduced to education through U3A and perhaps
become 'regular' students.

They invited a number of people who had registered their
interest to a day conference and the result was that four retired
people, from different areas in the county, volunteered to try and
introduce the U3A idea into their home locales. Peter Grainge
drew up some guidelines to assist them in making a start and it
was agreed to meet again in about six months to discuss progress.
So far it looks as if the efforts of the local organisers has produced uneven results. The notion is that local groups will develop
quite independently according to the needs and resources of the
area, but that they will be linked into a county network to derive
whatever benefit they can from mutual support, activities and
exchanges. It is still too early to see if this system will succeed
but it does seem to be on the right track. This sort of network,
which capitalises on small, local groups as the foundation, may
be the only one that can work. The style of the U3A should be
such that it makes opportunities readily available to older people
wherever they happen to be.

London and Devon are another pair of areas with large,
scattered populations, but both seem to have developed a strong
central base which will act as the administrative centre to
co-ordinate and service the many local groups. It must be
admitted that these examples, and that of Sussex, are very
fortunate in that they have, to differing degrees, independent
funding and positive support from an established institution.
In the case of Sussex the idea is being promoted by professional
staff within the parameters of their own department. London
and Devon are, to some extent, independent wings of larger
organisations. A more detailed case study of Devon is in
chapter eight. In London the U3A is supported by a grant from the
Voluntary and Christian Service Charity, and was run from an
office at the University of London in the department of Extra-
mural studies, by a full time administrator on a year's secondment

from the Polytechnic of North London, plus a large number of
voluntary workers. At this point in time it is difficult to envisage
how the network approach, obviously so essential to areas with
the kinds of demographic characteristics outlined above, could
work without a substantial input of funds to support the central
service mechanism. There seems no reason why such a
mechanism could not be operated by volunteers, but the costs of
communications, in whatever form, are high and cannot be
avoided.

In contrast, 'self-contained units' whether they be of thirty or
so members as in Harpenden or 500 as in Cambridge are able to
support themselves through subscriptions and concessionary rents
or freely given premises. The necessary expenses of photocopying of newsletters or information circulars, postage, tele-
phone or refreshments at meetings, are being met out of the
members' pockets. So far no U3A has successfully solicited funds
from local firms or industry. 'Starter grants' have been obtained,
in one or two cases, from Age Concern England's Operation
Enterprise and, as mentioned, the U3A National Committee has
been able to help in a few cases of individualsoperating completely
on their own during the first stages of publicising the idea.

The Manpower Services Commission, as U3As Mid-Wales and
Lancaster have found may certainly be a possible source of funds
for those groups which can present an attractive package of
opportunities for older people, especially if they are catering for
the older unemployed workers. It has always been understood
that each local group will be responsible for undertaking to raise
its own revenue as a part of its activities. There are still strong
feelings in some groups that no members should be asked for
more than a few pence per session, to cover immediate costs,
such as tea or coffee. Others, such as the Cambridge group,
feel that members want to make a financial commitment, on the
basis that if you pay for something, you value it more. Its £20
annual subscription is by far the largest, with most groups asking
for something less than £5 per year or alternatively, a sessional
fee of around twenty five pence.

As each local group grows and diversifies into more and
varied activities, obviously their administrative structures will
become more complex. Cambridge has now reached the stage of
being 'governed' by a committee elected from the semi-annual
meeting of Life Members. It is understandable that in an enterprise such as the U3A committees or working parties should
consist, first of all, of people who volunteer or are asked to
participate, rather than members elected by the group. It is
assumed that, as memberships increase, local groups will all

reach a level of maturity where they will be democratic in their choice of leaders and in the making of decisions on all matters pertaining to their activities.

During the summer of 1983 the Third Age Trust was registered with the Charity Commissioners. The Objects of the Trust are listed as 'the advancement of education, and, in particular, the education of middle aged and elderly people'. The Trust will be governed by a Council which will include the members of the National Committee for the University of the Third Age (who will ultimately be subject to election) and Councillors representing all affiliated local groups. Local groups will be free to choose whatever name they please, without having to include either 'university' or 'third age' in the title. Any local group may apply to the National Committee for affiliation. They will be represented by a person chosen from a properly established committee or group of officers, or from the group as a whole. Each local affiliated group will be eligible for charitable status. This move should, among other things, facilitate the raising of funds at the local level.

Communications between members is vital to any successful programme. Several local groups now print and distribute their own newsletters giving details of courses and other activities. U3A London has launched its own magazine with a wide range of literary and practical contributions from members. In a venture where individual study groups are meeting regularly, there does need to be some method of ensuring the feeling of belonging to a wider movement. At the local level the newsletter can achieve this result, as well as providing much needed information. The same applies on the national level. For the first year or so of its life the national movement lacked a feeling of cohesiveness. It was possible to visit groups who knew nothing of the existence of similar groups in other parts of the country. An informal newsletter was distributed to organisers from August 1982 but too often the information it contained on new developments never reached the actual members. A movement like the U3A must rely for impetus on the spirit of its members. They are pioneers but they do need to know that they are not alone. Also, because of the diversity of the programmes undertaken, there is a great deal to be learned from looking at what others are doing. So, in September 1983, the National Committee introduced 'The Last Post......the Newspaper of the U3A and Associated Groups'. Distributed free to thousands of members throughout the country, the paper itself was greeted with enthusiasm but its title, thought by a few to be a rather witty play on words, was roundly condemned by the majority. The paper will become a regular feature as long as the local members are prepared to support it. It will be re-christened but otherwise continue much as it started, as a vehicle for exhibiting local group news, expounding relevant views and exploring many areas of interest to all U3A members.

It is possible to imagine a future where Third Age Learning Centres are dotted around the country, being run entirely by and for the benefit of retired people. However, for the time being, groups meet wherever they can. In a small town outside Lancaster a group meets in school rooms while the children are at games. In Wakefield meetings are held in the local Library. In Yeovil the HQ for the U3A is a room over the swimming baths and in Stevenage the Leisure 50 group meets at various institutions. Some activities are also taking place in peoples' homes, which seems a logical way to provide educational activities on a small scale. It also answers the expressed object of providing oppor-tunities for those who for whatever reason are unable to leave their homes or get about with ease. The U3A in Bristol has also stated its intention of providing educational activities for the housebound and may even arrange one-to-one exchanges to take place in people's homes. The National Committee is hoping to encourage this kind of experiment.

While activities have developed freely in different centres according to peoples' needs and resources, there is a pattern emerging which seems to exemplify the shape of U3As to come. Cambridge, Saffron Walden, London, Harpenden, Stevenage, Lancaster and others all have programmes that include a regular general meeting and/or lecture as well as smaller, specific study groups. The focus of the small seminar groups depends entirely on the interests and expertise of the U3A members and their willingness to act as leaders. The initiative may come either from an individual offering to lead or tutor a group in a subject of their choice or from the knowledge that there are x number of people who want to study a certain topic. It is then up to the organisers to find a suitable leader and a venue.

The earliest analysis of subjects-wanted was made from those first letters which came in response to Eric Midwinter's broad-cast in July 1981. The subject asked for most often was English literature with others requesting creative writing, poetry and quite basic English or English grammar. History was second on the list, including social, medieval, Roman, modern and local. A smattering expressed an interest in politics, current affairs, sociology and philosophy. Various languages were requested and, in the arts, suggestions ranged from jazz piano to art and music appreciation. Two people wished to study theology while one wanted to go hill walking. Those asking for subjects in the

scientific or technical fields were few and far between. The
questionnaires sent out to all prospective participants in the
Cambridge Easter School reinforced the picture of an emphatic
interest in the arts and humanities with little interest in science
or technology. However, in practice, there does seem to be
some desire to look at topics in this latter area. Gardening,
both practical and historical, is popular but perhaps the area
where there is the greatest growth of interest is in computer
studies. 'Looking at the Stars' is a popular course in Yorkshire
and involves the members in skywatching. The Harpenden group
enjoy a visit to British Aerospace; the Stevenage group have
heard talks on bees while Cambridge offers 'The Plant in Relation
to East Anglian Environment' as well as a course on nutrition.

Languages are understandably popular, with the more predictable ones being supplemented by Serbo-Croat and Chinese. One
or two groups have already arranged exchange visits with
Université du Troisième Age groups in France and it is hoped
that this interest in language as an area of study will lead to many
connections being forged with similar groups in other countries.
Study tours may also take the opportunity of looking at other areas
of interest such as culture, politics, art, architecture and so on.

In the arts there is also a wide range of interest from the
appreciative to the practical. Many U3A members have started
to develop talents and skills that they never knew they had. In
Buckfastleigh in Devon such a high proportion of their members
have developed or revealed an interest in arts and crafts that they
are hoping to open their own shop to sell their products to tourists.
Cambridge found that their recent exhibition of art was a good
showcase for interesting the general public in what the U3A was
doing.

(E) Stage Five. The Diversification Process.
Whatever the subject matter, the style of U3A study recognises
the needs of people in this particular generation to socialise with
others who have similar interests, outlooks and problems. It is
therefore not surprising that having come together, they soon find
they have other things in common which leads to the organisation
of further activities. In some cases different types of activities
have arisen simultaneously but what most people would call
'recreational' or 'leisure' pursuits are now included in many U3A
programmes. Rambling, cycling, swimming, yoga, short tennis
and other games are available. Organised walks are sometimes
combined with local history investigations or the study of gardens.
More sedentary activities such as scrabble, bridge and chess
have also found takers. This kind of activity neatly demonstrates
the 'free form' of the University of the Third Age idea. The

members of the group take the opportunities for expansion, change, new directions and stimulation, wherever they see them without being bound by any preconceived notions or strategies of 'the course'.

In the smaller Third Age groups such as Yeovil and Saffron Walden, recreational or leisure opportunities are just one segment of the whole spectrum planned by the organisers. Where greater numbers are involved, as in Cambridge, a separate or sub-committee takes the responsibility of arranging activities, venues and so on. This is symptomatic of a new stage of development. The philosophy of the U3A is about sharing...... whether it is a sharing of resources, information, experience or skills. It is certainly about the sharing of responsibility. The one notable failure of a U3A, the initial attempt to get activities off the ground in Sussex, occured for this reason. The enthusiastic, well-motivated initiator seemed incapable of sharing the responsibility or of taking a share of the experience and knowledge of others. We have to expect and anticipate problems of this nature and, as always, we have learned something from the experience. They are probably inevitable in any organisation where volunteers are asked to come forward to help get a new idea off the ground. Perhaps the situation of those involved in U3A makes it particularly vulnerable. Here we have a group of people who have, in retiring, relinquished what might be called their 'power base'. A few will inevitably feel an uncontrollable urge to fill that gap. Others, hopefully the majority, will find fulfillment in the co-operative exercise of their experience.

As the educational and other 'offerings' increase, and the membership grows, so the administrative structure will become more complex. Ideally this development should be seen as an increase in the opportunities for participation of more and more individual members. As more 'jobs' need to be done, then more of their skills will be employed. The superstructure should develop horizontally rather than vertically.

At the moment four areas have their own U3A offices. London has a full-time Academic Administrator and a large rota of volunteers. The office is located in the Department of Extra-mural studies at the University of London. Cambridge has an office for which it pays a modest rent. It is now staffed by a part-time paid secretary and many volunteers, although, as was mentioned earlier, the Committee has decided they do need more paid help. In Mid-Wales a space for a U3A office has been given by the Montgomery College of Further Education and in Devon the TAP office is financed by their foundation grant.

In Bristol, Manchester, Lancaster and Sussex, the point of

contact and liaison for U3A activities is the office of various
members of staff in an Adult Education Centre, extra-mural
departments and a College of Further Education. Although the
promotion of U3A is openly supported by these departments, in
most cases, separate budgets for expenses do not exist and
funding may be 'hidden'. This is also true in the cases of one or
two other centres where the initiative is at a very early stage.
In about one dozen places all the U3A activities are administered
by people from their own homes.

Peter Laslett's original 'Objects and Principles' place
considerable emphasis on research on two fronts. Principle
Thirteen states:

'Every member will be encouraged to join in the widespread
accumulation of scattered data required for advancement in
knowledge of certain kinds (for example archaeology, natural
history, the history of population and social structure, the
history of climate and geological events). Every member
will be expected where possible to have a research project
of his or her own, and to write up the results.'

Research of this kind cannot be separated from other academic
pursuits as most members will at some time or another be
expected to make presentations to their study group and in the
course of so doing will have used research techniques. The
Harpenden group have been helped by one of their members, a
retired tutor-librarian, who has produced useful notes on
information retrieval using the local library resources. Apart
from the obvious benefits of getting knowledge through these
methods, the encouragement of research will undoubtably open
up new ways of learning to many older people who in their past
educational lives have experienced little beyond the more
sedentary styles of learning.

The second kind of research to be nurtured is referred to in
Principle Nineteen.

'Apart from the voluntary research undertakings of its members
on every suitable subject, the university shall seek to set up
professional research activity into the process of ageing,
especially as a social phenomenon.'

This Principle has already lead to the formation of three research
groups. In Saffron Walden they are planning research into
'migration' in retirement and housing problems in their area.
They have already made contact with an expert in this field and
he will speak to the U3A and offer them guidance.

The Cambridge Research group, under the guidance of Peter
Laslett, completed their first project some months ago. They
monitored all four television channels for one week and have

subsequently been analysing the images of the aged and ageing discovered therein.

In Oxford a research project is being set up in conjunction with community education workers to examine the educational and leisure needs of elderly people in one area of Oxford and to look at how these needs can best be met, with particular reference to a day centre in that area.

The embryonic group at the University of Surrey hoping to start a U3A network in that county is currently mooting the interesting idea of researching the development of the U3A in Surrey as it actually happens. All these projects have exciting prospects. Far too little research is undertaken in this country in the area of social and educational gerontology. Financial stringency makes it highly unlikely that professional bodies will be able to change this state of affairs much in the near future. Who better then, to open up this area, than the retired themselves, with in many cases, the interested support of the professionals? Not only will the actual work be stimulating to those involved, but the consequent knowledge gained will most certainly benefit a very wide public.

(F) Stage Six: The Future Potential

The picture of current activity gives a hopeful vision of future development. Individuals take the initiative, involve others and a new group comes into being. Having discussed the idea and its relevance to local conditions, they introduce it to a wider public. People begin to commit themselves to turning the idea into reality. Information is gathered about who wants to do what, where it can be done and whether it actually happens! More and more people with more and more skills, and more and more needs, become involved as the network grows. More questions are posed...... more answers found.

No one can say what will be the ultimate form of the University of the Third Age in Britain. Quite likely there will be no ultimate form. It will go on growing and changing as the needs and resources change. Within the foreseeable future though, it is possible to predict various developments, some of which are extension of activities already underway.

Over the next few years many new groups will arise at local level. If, as seems likely, the local group is the most appropriate form for Third Age learning then it is possible to imagine thousands of such units covering the country. Each will offer a variety of study groups, weekly or fortnightly general meetings or lectures, opportunities for the participation of the housebound or less mobile, research activities, both for individual pursuits

123

and into wider areas of relevant interest, sporting and recreational activities, general social opportunities such as the luncheon
clubs now functioning in Cambridge and Saffron Walden, outings,
to places of interest and to cultural and other events......in fact,
any kind of service which the local group feels it might offer,
including advice on other forms of educational opportunities
supplied by other providers.

But these groups will not operate in isolation. There will be
regional networks such as those already developing in Sussex and
Lancaster. There will be opportunities for Third Agers to take
part in courses and activities put on by other providers, such as
the scheme being launched in London whereby London U3A members
are kept informed of chances to participate in short courses on a
variety of topics at various institutions throughout the capital.

There must be a strong national body whose function will be
primarily one of liaison and service. The development of a
national newspaper for the U3A and allied groups is vital to the
growth and maintenance of a universal spirit. It is also an
essential tool for the local groups. A further development will
be a journal, published at intervals and dedicated to the exhibition
of research findings, and creative 'produce' of U3A members.

As has already been mentioned, exchanges, usually for the
purpose of practising languages learned, have been undertaken and
always include social and other learning opportunities. This is an
area where great expansion is possible. Many local British U3A
groups will want to offer their members the possibilities of
travelling abroad and meeting like-minded people from other
countries. They will, of course, have to be prepared to host
groups on their home territories. The focus of such tours need
not be language at all, but may bring together students, for
example, of archaeology, to make joint explorations, or
enthusiastic walkers who may want to ramble in distant fields
with foreign friends.

Another function that a national body can perform is to organise exchanges within this country. These may take two forms.
It is hoped to be able to compile a list of lecturers, tutors or
group leaders, who are experts in any number of different
subjects. These individuals would then be invited to visit
another U3A group either for a single lecture, a series of talks
or a session of workshops. Their fares would be paid by the
host group who would also offer accommodation, perhaps in
members' homes, to keep the costs as low as possible. In this
way the emerging expertise and experience of U3A members can
be made available to a wider public.

Secondly, whole U3A groups may wish to make exchanges.

A group from London may want to visit Lancaster to make a
study of flora and fauna in the Lake District while students of
drama at Nottingham may appreciate a few days at the Festival
Theatre in Chichester, and some system may be devised for
organising reciprocal hospitality.

The lessons learned from observing the development of new
groups needs to be continually re-assessed and re-distributed to
new initiators. The U3A DIY has already gone some way towards
fulfilling this service, but it will need constant updating. There
are possibilities for producing other kinds of materials that will
be useful to the successful launching and maintenance of groups.
There is very little material available in this country on 'group
dynamics' and the vital techniques of keeping a group balanced
and productive. The National Extension College now has a unit
promoting useful exchanges between study circles and a fruitful
link may be forged with the U3A. Again, there are many
possibilities including the development of courses for group
leaders, or the production of video cassettes and/or printed
material which would be designed to help individuals overcome
the problems which inevitably arise in self-help groups.

In our press release heralding the launch of U3A DIY we also
announced another development, labelled as 'a formula that could
enrich the lives of Britain's rapidly increasing elderly population'.
This anticipated active liaison with the new Channel Four programme 'Years Ahead', but has still, after more than a year,
not been fulfilled. Our press release spoke of encouraging U3A
groups 'to set up study circles to use the documentary features
as a basis for discussion and research'. We also hoped that U3A
groups would become actively involved in contributing to the
'OutrAGEous' media watch feature (seeking out examples of
ageism) and using the 'Years Ahead Noticeboard' feature.
However, there has been a general lack of interest in the
programme from U3A members and what we termed as an
'opportunity to participate actively in this major television series
for older people.... which exemplifies the spirit of the University
of the Third Age' has not been taken up.

However, we do try and continue to encourage U3A groups to
use television and radio material in general as a basis for their
study groups. This may be one answer to the increasingly raised
problems of providing sufficiently stimulating activities in remote,
rural areas. The new edition of U3A DIY, published in September
1983, has a Media Page explaining the various ways in which
groups can use what is available and how they can make contact
with producers and providers. We have also arranged for local
groups to receive on a regular basis the publications of both

Independent and BBC Continuing Education departments.

Whatever shape and dominion the national Third Age body takes on will be entirely dictated by its grass roots. Direction will be imposed from below, and services developed at the request of local groups. The one prerogative that <u>may</u> have to come from the centre is a duty to remind the local groups that they are part of a national and possibly international network, to encourage, if not nag, them into accepting and fulfilling a 'duty' to older adults in general. The sight of large numbers of retired people actively and happily involved in broadly defined 'educational' activities, benefitting from programmes that they have planned themselves to meet <u>their</u> needs and make the most of <u>their</u> resources, and backed up by their own research findings, can only make the general public more aware that this form of activity is not only suitable but highly beneficial, not just for those with previous adult educational experience but for the great majority of older people.

And, as a final 'nationwide' pronouncement, it is worth noting that, as of the spring of 1984, there were, in Britain, over fifty U3A groups, in one or other of the five stages of development, involving a total membership of over 4,000 people.

Chapter 8

THE UNIVERSITY OF THE THIRD AGE IN CAMBRIDGE

VERNON FUTERMAN

Vernon Futerman was educated in Berlin and Paris and
has held high executive posts in manufacturing industry.
Having retired early, he has devoted himself totally to
the successful U3A in Cambridge, for which he is the
Director of Studies.

This is to be a factual report on the history and development
of the University of the Third Age in Cambridge, from its
beginnings to the present day, although it will of course become
essential at certain points in the narrative to dwell briefly on the
schools of thought that have pervaded the whole aura of U3A.

The first major public meeting to discuss the possibilities of
establishing the U3A idea in this country was held in Cambridge
in June 1981. From this meeting arose what eventually became
the first committee. They set about planning the so-called
'March Week' or 'Easter School'. This was a six day period at
the end of March 1982 conceived as a trial balloon to prove the
workability of self-help seminars. About 75 people enrolled,
25 from outside Cambridge, and were asked to fill in a
questionnaire listing interests and experience. With this
material the organisers allocated people to study groups, ranging
in size from 5 to 15 and covering a wide range of topics, and
selected people to make presentations in the seminars on
different days. The result was concensus of opinion on the
positive nature of the experiment with the proviso, expressed by
a majority of the participants that, in future, a more structured
formula should be applied to the aspect of U3A rather than a
completely 'anarchic' free for all which would not lend itself to
the more serious intentions of study of many of the members.

Beyond the fact that there was a definite demand and need
expressed for this type of self-help institution, nothing else was
clear and obvious. As a result of the Easter School a number of

new people were co-opted onto the committee and we began the
process of deciding just how to proceed. Certain principles soon
crystallised into definite guidelines for the programme to be
achieved. We hoped to begin in October of the same year and
that meant that there was precious little time for preparing a
'syllabus' committing tutors and speakers and, worst of all, for
booking rooms and halls as venues for all these activities. In
addition, in order to attract members we had to have an enrolment drive and that had to be prepared for with a publicity
campaign.

In the course of the ensuing weeks three streams of
activity were planned for Cambridge. Firstly, a series of
weekly lectures to be called 'Foundation Lectures', as they were
to serve as the foundation for particular pursuits of interest and
might later on be followed by a series of seminars on the same
or allied subjects. The name was also chosen because these
lectures could be considered as being of fundamental interest to
the philosophy of mind extension that was to be accepted as one
of the tenets of our organisation. Luckily, we had in Cambridge
sufficient eminent scholars and thinkers who were only too happy
to give us their time and let us share a little knowledge with them.
The framework of the lectures was to be entirely informal. They
were, and still are, being held on Wednesday afternoons and take
the following format: The meeting is opened by an 'official' of
U3A, usually a member of the Executive Committee, utilising
this opportunity to announce any communication, arrangements
or future plans. As a very large number of members attend,
this can truly be called a meeting of the 'university'. This
platform was most important in the first year of our existence as
our only means of communication. After the announcements, the
Chairman introduces the speaker whose talk, frequently accom-
panied by slides or other illustrations, will last approximately
one hour. The weekly lectures have been so enthusiastically
received that people have come to regard them as a regular
Cambridge event and allow for them in planning their diaries.
There are usually non-members of the U3A present as the
lectures are advertised in the local papers' 'What's On' Column.
Non-members now pay an entrance fee as an accepted routine.

Secondly, a programme of weekly seminars, covering a wide
range of topics and usually taking a period of ten weeks is the
second stream of academic activity. After the first term, which
was in many ways experimental but nonetheless very successful,
a lot of the original seminars such as History of Art, Political
Science, Music, English Literature and so on, were carried
forward and are even now still running. Others had to be

terminated after the first term for various reasons, such as the
non-availability of a tutor, and were replaced by new ventures,
always maintaining an average level of between 35 to 40 different
seminars every week. This includes Fine Arts classes which
started with a class in sculpture and to which, at the beginning of
this year, a Painting and Drawing class was added.

Since the beginning of the 1983/83 academic year, when it was
obvious that U3A Cambridge was here to stay, it has been our aim
to run classes and seminars on a long term structured basis.
For instance we have now started a Modern English Literature
course with a syllabus covering at least two but possibly three
years, beginning with Thomas Hardy, followed by Joyce and so
on. Another new venture is going to be a Drama and Acting
seminar which we hope might lead to the formation of a Dramatic
Society .... U3A Mummers or Grand-Mummers?

Thirdly, there is our Language Workshop of which we are,
with some justification, very proud. With a maximum of eighteen
classes in different languages and/or differing levels of
proficiency per week, we think we are one of the largest foreign
language teaching institutions in the UK. The range of classes is
enormous covering, at one end, Mandarin Chinese and, at the
other, Ancient Greek. In between lie the obvious and popular
modern European languages at all levels of fluency, Modern
Greek, Russian, and we can now add Serbo-Croat. There are
also two classes in Latin.

In order to complete the academic picture, we have, since
U3A started in Cambridge, formed a sub-committee to concen-
trate on Research. The first study undertaken by the group was
on 'The image of the elderly' as portrayed on television. A
report of the findings has now been published. Other activities
are being planned by the Research Group. They are considering
the setting up a separate Media Study Unit which could do work for
outside bodies requiring that sort of help with their own monitoring. There has already been some response to the idea and it
certainly offers tremendous scope in an entirely different
direction to our other functions.

The establishment of our own Newsletter should be seen as
part of the intellectual exercises of our institution, but it is, in
fact, much more than that and has, with the few issues so far
produced, caught the imagination of our members and assumed
by now a fundmental need for communication that has dwarfed the
most optimistic forecast. It has taken the courageous and
certainly well-meaning efforts of the individuals on our committee
to launch this Newsletter. However, although the issues produced have been useful and important, we have discovered two

areas of deficiency: one is a concerted effort to establish an editorial policy and the other is the organisation of a distribution system. The latter, in view of our inability to fund a regular posting of newsletter to all members (approximately 500 at the moment) has been the most difficult to overcome.

An Editor was appointed to edit and collate the various articles, news items, reports etc. supplied by members. The problems of the first printing and subsequent distribution has to be overcome. We had, some time ago, afforded ourselves the luxury of purchasing a second-hand electric typewriter and this provided us with the stencils from which a local, non-profit printing co-operative produced our Newsletter and other items, such as the programmes of courses.

In the meantime, a newly formed Community Services Group, which had a number of varied but important functions, analysed our membership list and produced, by appealing for volunteers, a group of people willing to distribute the Newsletter in their 'arrondissement'. A very few copies still have to be posted out to people in outlying districts or Life Members living outside Cambridge but this did not break the bank. Thus we have established a really satisfactory and close communications system with our members. We feel this is one of the main achievements of the year. The fact that we are going to have these regular contacts with members also means that we shall be able to keep in touch with housebound people, and perhaps learn if and when it becomes necessary to act as a link with members who require help and assistance, without in any way interfering with their independence. It has taken a long time to establish this network and it is by no means perfect but we are improving it and learning all the time. For instance, a system is required to add and change addresses of members moving in and out of our ranks. All this has to be dealt with in the most efficient manner as a disappointed member is one who, in Cambridge, receives his copy of the Newsletter a day later than his or her friend in another part of the city.

Another series of ventures, closely connected with the Community Services Committee, is at present only in the planning stage. It is hoped to set up a 'Befriending Service', to be available to members during periods of bereavement and other personal difficulties. It is only natural that an organisation such as the University of the Third Age should see this sort of function as one that comes naturally and will be a very important part of our service to members.

It is worthwhile noting that we have already established seminars held in the homes of housebound tutors. The first one to start this series was a study group looking at the History of Apartheid in South Africa. The tutor is a lady, Mrs Franklin, who had lived for many years in that country and on returning to this country and settling in Cambridge became an enthusiastic member of the Cambridge U3A but found, because of her disabilities, that it was difficult for her to attend seminar groups. She therefore offered to lead a group on a subject with which she was concerned and knowledgable, to take place in her own home. The Fine Arts Group also deserves particular mention. The Painting group started with two pupils and now has more than twenty, which means running three sessions per week to cope with the demand. It is symptomatic of the tremendous response by Cambridge to the Third Age idea that an exhibition put on by the Fine Arts Classes and staged at the Central Library, proved to be an enormous success. The Mayor and Mayoress of Cambridge were among many other leading dignitaries who attended the preview. When the idea of the exhibition was first mooted, many other sections of U3A asked to be allowed to join in and display examples of their work. Among them were the Chinese study group who presented brush painted or written Chinese poems and there were poems produced by our 'Writers' Circle'. A small showcase made up by our Nutrition Seminar contained diet study sheets, recipe books and other artifacts, showing how eating habits have changed over the past decades. A collage of photos depicted a trip to Hadrian's Wall undertaken by the History group.

These are, in brief, the major academic activities in Cambridge. We are however, running other activities which may be looked at separately.

We encourage individual groups to undertake their own ventures into the country or even, as happened recently, abroad. Our Travel Club, jointly with the French study circle, arranged a week's tour to the Loire Valley in France. They were welcomed by a local branch of the Université du Troisième Age, thanks to a liaison arranged between our senior French tutor and the corresponding group in France. We intend to extend these kinds of outings, based on the interests of different study groups, and feel they will become more successful than just the usual travel club ideas.

We have a very active Social Activites group in Cambridge which is comprised of a number of sections. The main Social Committee is responsible for organising visits to theatres and other functions. This has been very successful and has so far offered regular trips to the National Theatre in London and to Stratford on Avon and other places. The Committee has also

131

been responsible for the larger functions, such as our annual
Christmas Dinner held at one of the Colleges in Cambridge.

An offshoot of the main group consists of a band of volunteers
who run smaller functions such as Tutors' Receptions. These
are particularly important in a situation like we have here in
Cambridge where literally dozens of scholars, professors and
other voluntary teachers give so much of their time to the
University of the Third Age and the only time for meeting everyone engaged in the running of the organisation is this twice-yearly
get-together. In the summer it is in the form of a Garden Party
and in the winter we have a Christmas drinks party. This helps
to cement the close relationships needed to continue the great
work done by everybody and enables us to say thank you.

The Sports section has now been established for six months.
There is a gathering once every week in the local Sports Hall
where from 12 to 20 people meet to play short tennis, squash,
table tennis and so on, or to do yoga. Although normally
ignored by the local press, this group has caught the imagination
of the Cambridge newspaper who have done a very complimentary
write-up. We consider it very important, for reasons which are
obvious, to foster the physical activities of our institution and we
are trying to persuade larger numbers to take part. We do have
a separate swimming section in which the numbers are mounting
all the time, with currently over 40 participants, and we are
finding it difficult to cope with their enthusiasm.

The first term in 1983 saw the start of another new venture.....
a Luncheon Club. This is really a social club that meets in a
local hall once a week over a home made snack-lunch, for the
purpose of exchanging news and simply getting together. This
has proved to be highly popular and we have now connected a
Chess Club to it which takes place in the same premises
immediately after lunch. The Chess Club was originally planned
as a monthly activity but demand has now turned it into a fortnightly meeting. A Bridge Club has also been recently
established.

At the close of the Easter Week in March 1982, participants,
and visitors from outside Cambridge, were invited to become
'Life Members' of the University of the Third Age in Cambridge.
The fee was £5.00. There are now well over 500 Life Members.
In addition, U3A local members who wish to participate in any
number of activities on offer are asked to pay an annual
subscription of £20.00. This can be paid in instalments or may
be waived in the case of personal difficulties. This forms the
basic income of U3A Cambridge and is used to rent and run the
small office, pay for correspondence and communications, and,

where necessary, pay rent on premises for activities. Besides
this, we have held two fund raising events during 1983, one a
very well attended garden party at which goods and teas were
sold and, the other, a stall in connection with the local 'Care
Bazaar' held in the Guildhall in Cambridge. The proceeds,
modest at this stage, are kept in a separate account and are
earmarked 'Building Fund'. This represents our hopes of in
future having a home of our own. At the present time we have
an office which is much too small for our needs. We continually
need to find and negotiate for the use of many different venues
for our activities. We are in a constant state of anxiety lest we
shall one day find that we can neither obtain or afford to obtain,
the kinds of rooms we need in order to continue to provide all
the activities outlined above. The running of our current
programme, in literally dozens of different locations throughout
the city, with only a handful of volunteers could be described as
being 'multi-phrenic', let alone schizophrenic. We pray that
this miracle will continue just a little longer so that a permanent
solution, both in terms of personnel and accommodation, can be
found. This is a constant theme of concern in our deliberations.

It always seems that this complicated administrative system
is something of a miracle. All activities are organised by
volunteers. A very elaborate Organisational Chart has been
drawn up based vaguely on personal administrative experience as
well as experience gleaned from other voluntary involvements.
I have tried to adapt this to the U3A where no precedent existed,
but, on the other hand, there is an enormous fund of goodwill
among the members. That goodwill has proved to be decisive and,
with a great deal of improvisation and inspiration, we managed to
make the University work along the lines originally envisaged.

Today we have reached the stage where a nucleus of permanent,
paid staff is essential to ensure the smooth running of the
organisation. It will consist of a half-time secretary, a part-
time Technical Assistant and an Administrator with experience
in education. At the time of writing, we have so far found only
our secretary. The Technical Assistant is the next step. This
will be someone with a car, capable of doing all the practical jobs
such as delivering posters, collecting material from the printers,
operating our projector and other equipment used in lectures,
preparing classrooms, moving blackboards and the thousand and
one other things associated with running a programme of this kind.
Finally we will appoint the administrator who will help with the
contact and liaison with tutors and seminars, the supervision of
classes, timetables and so on.

Chapter 9

THE THIRD AGE PROJECT IN DEVON

FRANK WATSON

> After joining the navy at fifteen and retiring thirty years
> later as lieutenant-commander, Frank Watson began
> research at the Dartington Institute into the needs of
> early retired and redundant workers. Now he is Director
> of the Dartington Third Age Project and Community
> Programme Agency, covering many groups and activities
> throughout South Devon.

A scheme funded by the Nuffield Foundation and the
European Social Fund in Totnes, Devon, differs considerably
from many other Third Age Groups. Originally the New
Horizons Project for Mature Redundant Workers and Early
Retired persons, the management committee was persuaded by
Michael Young not only to adopt the philosophy of the University
of the Third Age but also its title. Despite misgivings, this was
agreed, but without 'University', and chiefly because no member
of the committee could think of a better name. Today the 'Third
Age Project' is well known amongst the mature unemployed, but
is more popularly known as T. A. P. , although we have dispensed
with the logo showing that instrument and the associated drip.

The project aims to encourage self-help and self-reliance
amongst the mature unemployed and retired people. One may
ask who is considered mature and who decides? This is, of
course, an area for flexibility, or perhaps, more truthfully,
indecision. A guide line of forty plus was established but here
and there we do have some very young-looking mature people.
The date on the bottle does not always indicate a mature wine.

Initially the pilot project was to serve the towns of Totnes,
Buckfastleigh and Paignton, including the immediate rural areas.
Finding premises for the activities proved no problem. In
Totnes we rented some rooms as a base, to be open when needed,
at least from 9-5 Mondays to Fridays. Paignton provided two

community minded people, in the form of the Methodist Minister (formerly an industrial chaplain) and the Warden of the Community College. Both had premises suitable for our needs. Not only do we make full use of their premises, we make full use of their expertise as well. They really have contributed so much and become very involved. Buckfastleigh has a Y.M.C.A. which also has a very understanding and helpful caretaker.

That takes care of the original concept, but like any well nurtured plant - and the project was well cared for by Michael Young and the Dartington Institute - the seedling began to sprout sideshoots. There were even some seeds being carried on the air via TV and radio, to be planted in many parts of the country. There are now no fewer than nine other groups in Devon using a variety of premises. There are also eight groups in other parts of the country which have developed from the seeds grown in Devon, with many other contacts being made.

On several occasions we have been asked 'Could the principles of TAP be applied in an Urban areas?' One interviewer said our project was middle class, and would not work amongst the blue collar workers of the Midlands? The answer, I believe,is that it would work anywhere. With the right sort of motivation, it could be successful anywhere in the world, let alone the Midlands.

What does the Third Age Project do? It was set up to meet the need of the unemployed and the retired to achieve mutual self-help and reliance. There are just so many needs that, after two years, we are still identifying new ones. Initially, in November 1981, a survey was carried out amongst a hundred mature people who lived in the pilot area. The results of that survey showed that there were nine main areas of need. These were:- i. Support; ii. Information; iii. Training; iv. Education; v. Arts and Crafts; vi. Voluntary Work; vii. New Enterprises; viii. Transport; ix. Employment. The areas have not been listed in any supposed order of priority, because, to different people in different towns, there were so many factors affecting that priority. However, they are in some semblance of order.

i-vi.   are functions of the Third Age Project.

vii.   is covered by a Business Development Service.

viii.   led to the founding of the Dartington and Totnes Omnibus Company Limited.

iv.   was originally covered by an informal job brokerage, but now includes a placement agency under Community Programmes.

The whole concept has now become the Third Age Project, still aimed at the mature, but of necessity covering a wider age span.

TAP in Devon

Early in the initial survey it became obvious that a main
function of any project for the mature unemployed would be
support, whether that support was in the form of person to person
counselling, the formation of support groups, or just facilitating
social contact.

South Devon is a trap for mature redundant workers from the
Midlands and the North. They wish to perpetuate the holidays
they have enjoyed whilst still earning! What simpler than to sell
up and buy a smaller place in South Devon. The social security
payments are the same, north, east, south or west. Of course,
they can get seasonal work to supplement their finances or so
they think! This leads to a lot of mature people, in strange
surroundings, without family or friends and rapidly diminishing
savings. It also leads to the highest proportion of the population
drawing retirement pensions, more even than the south or south
east seaside resorts and lovely places like Scarborough. Over
thirty one per cent of the population around Torbay draw their
retirement pension. It is amazing the number who find that the
first real social contact in the area comes from a Third Age
Group. Initially with two counsellors, of very different backgrounds and training, the counselling service was strained to the
limit. Courses in basis counselling skills were organised and a
number of volunteers identified to help. No matter what importance we place upon counselling,and it has its place, like so many
other groups, the social contacts created or engineered prove
invaluable to most people.

Perhaps here is a good place to explain why there has been no
talk of members. There is no formal membership and anyone who
wishes to involve themselves is welcome. Many mature people
are fed up with the amount of irrelevant paper that comes through
their letter boxes and just do not bother to read the title let alone
the summary of what subject is covered. It seems that less of the
essential information is reaching those for whom it was intended.
Daily, often in the course of idle banter, a need for information
comes to our attention. Every group meeting produces numerous
requests for information and TAP now has a Resource and
Information Centre to meet this vital need. The TAP News which
is produced monthly has an increasing circulation. It is this
Newsletter that is intended as the corner stone of the Information
Service.

Training as distinct from education is something that mature
people seem willing to accept in small doses. What TAP has
found are certain areas where training is nominal but support
continuous and these areas fill a void in the average older persons
training. For example,our one day Self Presentation course

includes: How to set up a job search; Letters of application; Personal Information Charts or C.V.; Interview techniques. Ongoing support from this course has helped many to find employment. On our first course we had eleven people. In the plenary session the question was asked 'How many of us do you think will find employment within the next year,' The optimistic course organiser said six; today eight of that course are in full time employment.

Another area was bookkeeping for those who were producing goods at home for sale or were thinking of setting up a new enterprise. Many crafts people found that with the help of experienced accountants and bookkeepers they were able to present their books or accounts to likely sources of finance. Of course they had a far greater success rate than before. The training provided by other bodies was advertised in a way which appealed to the mature and many more are now deciding to take part in training schemes.

Education is on the whole well provided for by existing centres of learning in this area. It came as a slight surprise to find that to the mature in particular, adult education was considered: Middle Class; Middle Age; Middle of the road. It's now more popularly called 'the 3M service'. Much effort has been put into working with Community Colleges and Adult Education Centres to dispel that image. However, when a class of twelve comprises a solicitor, a dentist, an accountant, five teachers and two middle aged former professional ladies, it does take some encouraging to get a labourer and his wife to join. The involvement of people like Peter Grafton, Warden of the Community College, with our group in Paignton helps enormously to dispel prejudices.

With U3A this warning was sounded at Cambridge in March 1982 during Granada's filming of the Chalk Face programme. It seemed to be aimed at the middle class retired person. In fact on more than one occasion U3M has replaced U3A, that is: Upper Middle Class; Upper Middle Age; Up Market Academically. This is the prime reason that 'UNIVERSITY' was left out of this project title.

Many mature people, having left school at 14, were reluctant to return to what they thought may be classroom discipline. Sitting behind desks facing a black-board and teacher was to the vast majority less inviting than the telly or the pub. However, sitting around in a lounge listening to one of their 'friends' passing on knowledge is different, particularly between opening hours or before 'Crossroads'.

In our survey at the start of the project we had identified so many skills that mature people possessed; over 250 in fact.

Many were willing to share their skills with others. All they needed was opportunity, timing and a little encouragement. Amongst the skills now being passed on are: wood carving; pottery; knitting; glass engraving; painting in oils, pastels and water colours; marquetry; porcelain painting; gardening; house plant cultivation; local history; bookkeeping; creative writing; bridge; chess; DIY. Our French conversation group would be just as much at home across the Channel as they are in our lounge. Now they have decided to teach we 'English' their language. New groups for beginners at three centres are now active. There are many more one-off talks and we are sure many more learning groups will be formed. The will is there, the facilities are available, time has been a problem but with increased staff we look forward to our premises being fully utilised.

We should mention our computer group which although not as large as twelve months ago is still going. We started with five mature people. This grew as some brought along their children. At one time we had seventy five members from 11 years old to 76. We have now settled down to about twenty regular members age 13 to 68 in Totnes and another group in Brixham. Many of the subjects mentioned are in the arts and crafts. However, we defined those who wanted to learn or practice arts and crafts under the education banner. There were also many who wished to put their skills to more profitable use. These people meet regularly, arrange bulk purchase of materials, and take space to sell their wares at local fairs and shows. They even have their own market in the summer and for two full weeks at Christmas.

Surprisingly enough, we identified many people who wanted to undertake voluntary work. Until recently, placing them was a problem but now we are beginning to get voluntary bodies, in need of help, approaching us to assist. This is most gratifying because it is fulfilling a need on both sides. However, one never ceases to be amazed by 'man's humanity to man' - to hear 'So and so, how kind, I had such and such a problem and they helped me solve it'. That is really what the Project is all about, isn't it?

Third Age is a new enterprise but we identified so many other potential commercial enterprises that action was required. Initially we formed a group to discuss the ideas from which we identified four members who had no ambition to start a new enterprise themselves but did have a wealth of experience in business. These formed a consultancy group. Unfortunately we had seriously underestimated the demands upon their services. No volunteer could be expected to give quite so much. Further more, being a voluntary group they did not always attract official recognition.

The next step was to form an Enterprise Trust or as we have called it a Business Development Service with a full time, salaried Development Officer. This service has an advisory council comprising business and professional people, who still give their services for free when needed. Several new enterprises have developed as a result of this service providing over 40 jobs. There are currently fifty individuals receiving some form of help in addition to those who are already started. One recognises in rural areas that small new enterprises are the only way of finding new jobs.

In rural areas the problems of transport have grown over the past decade. As public transport is withdrawn so the cost of private transport has increased. Many have 'got on their bikes'; in fact Devon, never renowned for cycling, seems to be producing cyclists by the dozen, and of all ages. Car sharing is becoming common place, and particularly pleasing is the way those attending TAP activities have responded. However, for many an economic alternative to public transport was essential. Many community transport initiatives have blossomed and faded. Third Age joined with other interested parties to try and fill this gap. The result was a new bus service provided by the Dartington and Totnes Omnibus Co. Ltd. This 'community' bus company runs a regular service to villages in the North West of Totnes from 6.30 a.m. to 5.30 p.m. Mondays to Fridays including a special service for fifty schoolchildren. The average weekly numbers of passengers carried exceed three hundred and require two buses to maintain the services. At least seven villages would be without a transport service but for the Third Age initiative.

Last but by no means least we started an informal job brokerage service which had some success for a variety of reasons. Many employers were embarrassed by advertising jobs for mature people with so many youngsters unemployed. They are now being convinced to look for the right person irrespective of age. Using us as an agency saved management time and gave a reasonable guarantee of success.

'Ageism' as Michael Young says, is one of the fastest growing social problems of this decade. When applying for a job at the age of forty to be told 'Sorry you are too old' is not only disheartening, it is a disgrace. One of our problems is having to educate employers as to the value of experience and maturity.

Out of our desire to find work in the community for skilled hands we found the Manpower Services Community Programmes. They were looking for agents and, with our experience with the unemployed and the sponsorship of Dartington, we had the right pedigree. Our agency will have projects providing temporary work for one thousand long term unemployed by the end of 1983.

We recently applied to the Manpower Services Commission under its voluntary Projects Programme for funding for staff and materials to help us increase our activities. Fortunately our application was successful so we now have additional materials and staff which include a Resource and Information Centre Organiser, and extension officers with clerical support. The enquiries come in with pleasurable regularity and before long those associated with our project will be in four figures. Our target is to have numbers of local groups in three figures. Michael Young perceived the need several years ago and those involved with the Programme feel privileged in helping to meet that need.

Chapter 10

THE UNIVERSITY OF THE THIRD AGE IN SAFFRON WALDEN

JOHN JONES AND JOYCE MACELROY

John Jones, a retired deputy head teacher and writer on the history of the ballet, is now the research tutor of the Saffron Walden U3A. Joyce MacElroy has been a nurse, and physical training instructor and a Youth Play Leader: now she is the mainstay of the flourishing U3A in Saffron Walden.

Saffron Walden is a comparatively small country town in Essex which has been increasingly commuterised in recent years. Its long and varied history is mirrored in its buildings, street and school names: a ruined castle (decay not war), the largest parish church in Essex, a substantial Quaker presence and names such as de Bohun, Cromwell, Winstanley and R. A. Butler. There are well over two hundred clubs, societies and organisations serving the town and it is well provided with Evening and WEA Classes.

Joyce MacElroy, who was and is the mainspring of U3A activities in the town, was both fortunate enough and inquisitive enough to attend the Cambridge U3A Seminar in March 1982 and there she was very impressed by the idea of a learning/teaching relationship amongst Third Age people. Motivation was followed by action. Joyce talked to her many friends and acquaintances about the ideology of the U3A and found enough interest to call a preliminary meeting at the local library. There she explained the U3A concepts and found that the reception was mixed, but that there was enough support for her ideas to call a second meeting at the town's Youth and Adult Centre which was attended by a small delegation from the Cambridge U3A and about a dozen people from Saffron Walden. A small working party was set up and a series of monthly meetings was held. These meetings established that there was a clientele. Interests crystallised and the process of talent matching began. A framework for a programme of activities emerged and this was presented to

141

interested parties as a list of activities: there were more than
ten, and they were scheduled to begin in January 1983.

Before classes actually began, an Enrolment Day was
organised in the local library, one of the town's natural meeting
places. The local papers were alerted, one of them published a
picture of the oldest member signing on, not quite the sought-for
image, but by the end of the day there were more than fifty paid
up members and the range of activities had been extended. In
those first days, and since, Joyce MacElroy and her working
party, which was gradually elevated to the status of committee,
have enjoyed enormous support from individuals, from the Essex
Educational Authority, from the Warden of the local Youth and
Adult centre, from the Town's Librarian and from its Mayor and
from shopkeepers and others who have displayed U3A posters.
Joyce MacElroy was not only the instigator but the progress
chaser as well, visiting all the groups in turn, creating timetables, hiring and arranging rooms.

From the very beginning it was decided that the enrolment
fee should be kept to a minimum and that it should be the only
charge, its payment entitling people to attend all open meetings
and as many groups or classes as they wished. The fee for the
first year was set at £1 and to date there is every indication that
we can work effectively at this level. If there is any increase it
will be based upon room hire charges, each member of a group
contributing a small sum, probably ten pence per class attended.

Costs have been low because everything as been on a voluntary
basis; not even visiting speakers have been paid, and because we
have been very fortunate in that we have been charged only
nominal fees for the use of premises. The only substantial
hiring charge to date has been for a Day Centre for an Evening
Social, and that was met by a raffle. Secretarial expenses have
been paid. In addition to the enrolment fees we have received
£45 in donations.

To date the U3A in Saffron Walden has been a low cost
exercise, but growth brings its problems. Our membership
doubled in our first two terms. If this growth rate continues,
then problems of communication and accommodation are likely
to arise. To date, our communications have been by word of
mouth and by shop window advertising, reinforced by duplicated
timetables of the term's events and by the regularity of meetings.
Cancellations and re-arrangements are costly in terms of time,
money and frustration. We are already considering publishing a
newsletter, a development which will increase running costs.
The problem of accommodation, particularly for our monthly
meetings, is more pressing. We find that between a third and a

half of our membership attend monthy meetings and if our
membership were to double again we would be hard pressed to
find low-cost meeting places large enough to cope. However,
these meetings are essential to our organisation since they
create a sense of belonging, of loyalty, and are a focal point for
potential new members......'Come and see what happens. There
will be an enrolment fee of £1 if you decide to join'. They are
also of the greatest importance in keeping our members informed
of what is happening in the various groups, such as the Social
Group, which are continuously expanding their programmes.

Four groups have been chosen for close scrutiny. They are
an academic group, a discussion group, an art and craft group
and the research group. The criteria applied in making the
choice have been the representative nature of the group and its
illustration of the problems faced by the tutors.

The academic group is that studying German. The tutor, Mrs
Jean Pitt, writes:'the German group comprises five pupils. Of
the five, two are complete beginners and three have some previous knowledge of the language - a mixed ability group. However,
the non-beginners are willingly biding their time and refreshing
their memories whilst the beginners are taking their first steps.
As yet, nobody has dropped out. Fortunately, in view of the
degree of difficulty of the language, each student has a well
defined motivation to learn German and there is a genuine
commitment to doing work at home. In the absence of examin-
ation-type pressure, the atmosphere is most pleasant and
relaxed, a factor appreciated by both pupils and tutor. The
problems of teaching mixed abilities have not surfaced, due
largely to the intellect and personality of the pupils.'

The Discussion group has been more varied in membership
and, at its weekly meetings, tackles four or five topics, some
of which are inward looking, such as, 'Why did you join U3A?',
while others draw upon the experiences of the members of the
group, such as, 'What it is like living in Holland.' The tutor,
Mr Robert Whybrew, reports that most of the topics centre on
the local community and upon problems met by the members, but
matters of more general concern such as Unemployment and CND
have been discussed. The meetings are lively and the attendance
varies from four to seven.

Barbara Price-Smith, the Art Tutor, reports as follows:
'we started from scratch in the old art room of the Boys' British
School complete with easels and plastic palettes. Numbers have
fluctuated from a maximum of twelve to a minimum of three.
Members mainly wish to draw or paint but some four or five have
started working on both traditional hexagonal patchwork and the

Victorian 'crazy' variety. For the last three meetings, the group
has had to relinquish the Boys' British School (the site has been
sold for development) and has filled in with one meeting in a
member's house, which gave us a chance to work on roofs and
chimneys (the proverbial room with a view), one in the local
museum, which provided the members with a choice of subject,
and one in the Fairycroft Youth and Community Centre, which
will be our regular meeting place next term.'

The founding group included some who felt that, if the title,
'U3A, Saffron Walden' was to be used, then research must be part
of the whole. A Research Group was set up and its tutor, John E.
Jones, reports: 'our early meetings were spent considering what
to research. There was some talk of joining the U3A, Cambridge
research group and taking part in their 'Telewatch' which was
concerned with the way in which the older generation was por-
rayed on television, but it was decided, eventually, to investigate
the attitudes of the U3A generation to housing. The group sought
advice from Peter Laslett of Trinity College, Cambridge, and,
through him, of Professor Alan Lipman of the Welsh School of
Architecture. The choice was between a near replication of some
existing research to help develop research skills so that more
original work could be undertaken at a later date, and a more
novel approach which aroused the interest of the membership as
a whole. The latter course was decided upon. A questionnaire
was drawn up and ten members completed it. This experience
suggested that a more effective procedure would be to make the
questionnaire the basis of a structured interview, the interviewers
being given an instruction sheet. It is hoped that the interviews
will be completed next term. When this has been done it is
planned to produce a series of profiles based upon the interviews
which may or may not suggest common attitudes, experiences and
interests from which further lines of enquiry may develop. '

In May we were approached by a research worker from
Sidhartha Films to see if we were suitable material for a programme they were preparing for the Channel Four series,
'Years Ahead. ' Three meetings were held. In the first a small
cross section of members talked about why they had joined the
U3A and what they had got out of it. The second was a planning
session and included visits to the various locations that would be
used and the third was a briefing meeting. There was no script
as such but an awareness of the questions. Filming took place
over two days in June and the eventual television film showed
various groups in session, including the Keep Fit Class, the
Local History Study Group, the Art Group and the German Group.
There were interviews with five members, the organiser

(Joyce MacElroy) two tutors and two students. After all the excitement, the General Meeting which was held on the day the film was shown was the worst attended of the whole year, but we were given a video of the programme. The lasting impression was one of warm co-operation from all quarters and the members were charmed by the film crew. Reactions to the film itself were very varied and an informal report is being gathered for forwarding to the film company.

Social activities and discussions figure prominently in the programme. The Students' Union is every bit as important to the students as research is to the University. The monthly Luncheon Club is particularly popular: it is very pleasant to share a meal with friendly, articulate people. The Social Group have already organised visits to stately homes, walks and shopping trips and there is every indication that this aspect of the activities will both expand and diversify.

Our third ten-week term began on September 1983. It was advertised in shop windows and in public places. All our members and all those expressing an interest in our activities are invited to attend our monthly meetings. Recruitment has been steady since the end of last term. Many of our new members are recruited by existing members, but there is a U3A Information Desk on one afternoon a week in the local library.

In conclusion, it is worth summarising the main feature of the programme. It includes German, French, Spanish, art and crafts, local history, bridge, scrabble, and 'stroll arounds' and 'saunters', while, in private homes, are based French conversation, creative writing, play reading and the history of ancient religions. It is certainly a varied and tastily flavoured diet.

Chapter 11

THE UNIVERSITY OF THE THIRD AGE IN LANCASTER,
MORECAMBE AND DISTRICT

KEITH PERCY

Keith Percy is Organising Tutor for Extra-Mural Studies
at Lancaster University. An adult education specialist of
varied experience, he was instrumental in setting up the
Open College and Open Lectures schemes in Lancaster and
the north west.

Early in 1982, Margery Morgan, soon to retire from her post
as Reader in Literature at the University of Lancaster, and Keith
Percy, who was head of the small Extra-Mural Studies unit in the
University, made contact with the National U3A committee and
they agreed to do what they could to facilitate the establishment
of a U3A branch in the Lancaster area. The context appeared to
be appropriate: there was known to be a significant proportion of
retired people in the locality (particularly in the seaside resort
of Morecambe); apart from the two small towns of Lancaster and
Morecambe the population along the Lune Valley was distributed
in small villages poorly serviced by public transport; and since
its foundation in 1964 the University of Lancaster had sought to
foster close links with its surrounding community.
The University Extra-Mural Studies office had been in
existence since 1979 and had followed a clear policy of exploring
new ways in which the University's teaching and other resources
could be made available and useful to adult learners. The Open
Lectures scheme (through which members of the public were
encouraged to attend University undergraduate lectures free of
charge), the development of part-time first degree provision, and
the Summer Programme of holiday courses for members of the
public were examples of this policy. The Extra-Mural Studies
office regularly received from older people a variety of enquiries
about learning opportunities and dozens each year registered
under the Open Lectures scheme. As early as 1977 Keith Percy

had published the results of a small local research enquiry into education and the elderly which had emphasised the potential of older people themselves as a learning resource. This is K. A. Percy and J. G. Adams, <u>Education and the Elderly</u> (Lancaster Institute for Research and Development in Post-compulsory Education.)

Following newspaper stories and the distribution of leaflets, public meetings to promote interest in the U3A idea were held in Lancaster in May and June 1982. Those who attended were unanimous in their indignation at the patronising attitudes to the elderly which were prevalent in society and agreed that learning had an essential part to play in the active, healthy and happy life that many older people could, and wanted to, enjoy. They were unsure about the title 'University of the Third Age' but agreed that the attempt should be made to establish a local self-help learning association for older people, beginning with fortnightly afternoon social and discussion meetings taking place in Lancaster. They also accepted an offer by Keith Percy that his office would organise a (financially self-supporting) 'Study Day for Older People' on the University Campus to launch the local U3A association. This Study Day took place on 5 August 1982 under the auspices of the University's Summer Programme and 28 older people attended a programme of discussions/talks on local history, creative writing, microcomputers, yoga, natural history and other topics and some stayed into the evening to join in social events of the Summer Programme.

From September 1982 U3A in Lancaster and Morecambe took an established form. An executive committee was formed (membership was open to anybody who chose to come) with a chairperson who changed from meeting to meeting. Seven committee meetings were held in the first nine months. The first crucial decisions taken were that:

(i) emphasis would be on the formation of semi-independent study groups in Lancaster, Morecambe but also, emphatically, in the rural villages where formal adult education provision was normally limited and inaccessible.

(ii) a quarterly newsletter would be produced to serve as the communications backbone of the association.

(iii) there would be no concept of 'membership' as such - in other words older persons could attend any U3A meeting or study group free of charge on whatever basis they and the group found convenient. There would be an optional annual payment (£3 in 1982-3) but this was only levied to guarantee the receipt of the newsletter and to cover production and postage.

(iv) the title of the association should be allowed to evolve. For the time being it was decided to work under the title 'University of the Third Age' because of its national significance. In the event, throughout the period with varying degrees of enthusiasm, the committee continued to debate this title. It did not resolve the issue to its own satisfaction but, nevertheless, it grew to prefer that the Lancaster association be described under the more anonymous 'U3A' label rather than under the full-blown title of 'University of the Third Age'.

Keith Percy attended almost all meetings of the committee in a quasi-advisory capacity. More importantly, he made available to the association the services of one of the workers on a Manpower Services Community Enterprise Programme Project based in his office at the University. Such workers were recruited from the registers of the local long-term unemployed and were paid by the MSC to work, under the direction of a sponsor, on projects of benefit to the community. The project at the University was called OPAL (Opportunities for Adult Learning) and work with U3A was a relevant development of its brief. In November and December 1982 a young OPAL worker spent the equivalent of one working day facilitating and supporting U3A, acting as secretary of the committee, producing and distributing the first newsletter, receiving subscriptions and establishing a mailing list and helping to create the first rural study groups. This young worker left the project on appointment to a permanent post and, in January, was replaced by an older man who played a similar, but more extended, role (on the basis of approximately four working days per week) until June 1983.

By January 1983 the mailing list of subscribers to the U3A newsletter was approximately thirty strong and the mailing list of those who had expressed interest in U3A over twice as long. The committee laid emphasis on having a regular U3A Monday afternoon fortnightly open meetings in the restaurant of the Duke's Playhouse in Lancaster. Soon these meetings developed the practice of moving to a nearby room to hear a talk by an invited speaker (the OPAL worker arranged a programme of invited speakers from the University of Lancaster and from the community). Attendance at these meetings was never more than twenty, and often less, and the committee readily identified their primary problem, as a nascent and unfamiliar voluntary organisation, to be that of catching the public's eye, of promoting public awareness of their objectives and activities. The strategy adopted was that of orchestrating a press campaign in the local newspapers and on the local radio stations, but not before 'there was something on the ground' (that is, a range of U3A activities) about which the journalists could write.

In February 1983 a press release was issued which, among other things, advertised the establishment of nine U3A study groups in Lancaster, Morecambe and in villages and small towns to the north and east of Lancaster. Two of these groups had been functioning successfully for some months. The others were 'established' in the sense that an individual (normally an older person) had been found who agreed to lead one or more initial meetings around a particular topic or subject area in the hope that a study group could be formed which would develop its own dynamic and procedures. Meeting places were people's homes, community or adult centres and a local school. Topics or subject areas included creative writing, local history, music appreciation and literature. In no case was the exchange of money involved. There were no tutor fees because there were no tutors; there were no accommodation fees because the Extra-Mural Studies office and the OPAL worker successfully negotiated with the local authority and local centres that such fees were inappropriate; and thus there were no costs to be passed on to U3A participants as attendance/enrolment fees.

The February press campaign was very successful in the amount of press and local radio coverage achieved. Some of the press stories were of the nature 'Old Folks go Back to School'. Others more responsibly and accurately recounted the details of U3A largely in the words used in the press release. One or two articles latched emphatically and stridently on to the title of the association and clamoured insistently about a new 'University coming to Lancashire' or a 'new kind of University specially for the elderly'. The OPAL worker was the recipient of all requests for information about U3A and it was his task to inform interested enquirers about the Lancaster town meetings, the rural study groups, relevant activities of the University of Lancaster and other agencies and identify the potential for forming new study groups from those who wished to be associated with the scheme. The number of paid subscribers grew steadily and, in a variety of formats, seven of the nine study groups developed a continuing existence. One of the unforeseen consequences of the publicity was the incidence of enquiries from relatively far afield (South Cumbria coast, Fylde coast, Central Lancashire, Preston). There was no way in which a Lancaster-based voluntary assoc-iation could extend its interests over such long distances. These enquirers received polite and, as far as possible, helpful tele-phone calls or letters from the OPAL worker.

It is interesting that simultaneous with the emergence of the Lancaster and Morecambe U3A (which was essentially, at this

stage, a voluntary association receiving impetus and moral and
material support from a major educational institution and the
services of a paid worker temporarily employed in that institution) there was developing, a few miles away, the Caton and
Brookhouse Creative Leisure Activities Association.   The
association developed from the energy and persistence of a few
retired people in the villages of Caton and Brookhouse who were
determined to increase the provision of a variety of hobby,
special interest and social facilities available for older people,
and to ensure that there were sufficient opportunities locally for
older people to use their leisure time fruitfully.   Membership of
the association grew swiftly in early 1983, and dozens of older
people regularly attended afternoon meetings in which a range of
activities were organised.   The objectives of the Caton and
Brookhouse association were broader than those of U3A ('leisure'
rather than 'learning' - though in reality this distinction often
seemed more apparent than real); it had a defined concept of
membership (those who paid a membership fee); but - in its
entirely self-help and self-generating local nature - it provided
an instructive parallel for the Lancaster and Morecambe U3A.
In fact, the Caton and Brookhouse group came to occupy a form
of adjunct status to U3A.   A dozen or more members of the group
paid the U3A newsletter subscription and some leading members
of the Caton group regularly attended U3A committee meetings.
In fact, the Caton group perceived U3A as having more 'clout',
more negotiating strength, because of its links with the University
of Lancaster and with the national U3A movement - in particular,
with regard to achieving access to local authority accommodation.
     The success of the February press campaign proved to be
double-edged.   At a routine liaison meeting of local statutory
providers of adult education, held in the University of Lancaster
in March, it became apparent that some of the Responsible Body
and local authority agencies felt disquiet at some of the apparent
activities and considerable local publicity of U3A.   Keith Percy
offered to organise an informal meeting with members of the
local U3A committee for those providers who wished to attend.
The meeting duly took place in early April, with six members of
the U3A present and representatives of three Universities, three
local authorities and three areas of the WEA.   Among the issues
and concerns raised by the representatives of the statutory
providers present were
(i) possible confusions among potential adult students which might
be caused by the title 'University of the Third Age' and by local
U3A publicity
(ii) the question of 'standards' in U3A self-programming study

groups
(iii) the possibility that U3A might recruit participants who would otherwise have joined Responsible Body classes
(iv) the suggestion that U3A should not extend its activities beyond the immediate Lancaster and Morecambe area without prior consultation with statutory providers
(v) the fear that politicians might take a simplistic view of voluntary associations such as U3A which might affect the public funds available for provision of adult education.

On the other hand, certain of the representatives of the statutory providers present said that they were impressed by the vitality and development of U3A, that they believed strongly in the principles of self-help in adult education and that there were ways in which the development of U3A could be beneficial to statutory providers.

Before the informal meeting ended, members of U3A present offered to take back for discussion in their committee the possibility of an invitation to representatives of certain providers to attend U3A open committee meetings at certain key points in the year so that plans could be discussed (this was later agreed). Moreover, all present agreed to consider further the possibilities of mutual support; for example, that a U3A study group might (if an appropriate point were reached) be transformed into a WEA class or that a WEA class which failed to recruit a viable number could survive as a U3A study group.

By May 1983 U3A in Lancaster, Morecambe and area had reached a further plateau. Over a hundred older people were involved in the study groups and Monday meetings; about 50 were paying subscribers to the newsletter. The U3A committee had formalised itself with an elected chairperson, Nancy Cretney, and was examining a draft constitution. Its activities were quite well known nationally: Keith Percy was receiving regular requests from other parts of the country for information on how U3A-type associations could be established and on the kinds of relationship possible between U3A groups and other agencies. However, the committee had long known that in June 1983 the current phase of the OPAL Project would end and that, thereafter, there would be no MSC worker available to facilitate and to co-ordinate activities. Keith Percy had also indicated that his office would continue to support U3A as much as possible, but would leave initiatives to the association itself. The committee decided to ask the OPAL worker to organise in June a U3A Annual General Meeting, associated with some 'event' or 'Open Day' for older people, which would (hopefully) attract a large attendance and further press coverage. It would coincide with the end of the first year of existence of the local U3A and would, it was hoped, start off the second year with additional recruits and a renewed burst of activity.

Some obstacles were found to stand in the way of the June 'event'. An outcome of the disquiet among some of the local authority agencies which followed the February press campaign was that the local branch of NATFHE (the union for many adult and further education tutors) had expressed a wish not to co-operate with the local U3A association. The branch's grounds were that it feared that the development of free U3A study groups would affect the employment opportunities of part-time adult education tutors. The immediate effect of this NATFHE decision was that it proved impossible to find appropriate town centre local authority premises in which to stage the U3A 'event' and AGM. Thus, the 'event' was moved out to the University, three miles from the town centre and became the University of Lancaster 'Open Day for Older People' on 22 June 1983.

The 'Open Day' was a great success. A large-scale exhibition was organised of educational, social and leisure opportunities for older people in which the local U3A had three display stands to publicise the activities of study groups. A programme of short talks by University lecturers on their specialisms and visits to University departments was available. Towards the end of the afternoon representatives of local adult education providers were invited to speak about their provision for older people, and then the local U3A association held its AGM. Well over one hundred people travelled to the University for this 'Open Day' - yet more evidence of the felt need of large numbers of older people in this semi-rural area for extension of the opportunities for their involvement in learning activity from which cost, travelling difficulties, and administrative regulations about viable class sizes often debarred them.

It is too early to claim that the Lancaster, Morecambe and district U3A has succeeded or failed, and it would be similarly premature to make claims one way or the other, on the basis of the Lancaster experience, about the ideas which are given wide currency by the National U3A Committee, the Centre for Policy on Ageing and Age Concern.

Certainly one can say that some of the rural study groups near Lancaster worked well and provided worthwile social and learning experiences for participants. In one local history group, for example, U3A participants took turns at presenting their reading and research to each other, and in organising field trips and maintained a high level of activity and enthusiasm throughout

the year without the external support of 'tutors'. In a creative
writing group one experienced U3A participant took on the role
of convenor and tutor and within a few months one of the other
participants had succeeded in having her own work published.
The Lancaster U3A experience suggests that it is not possible to
be prescriptive about the form a study group should take, but
that it would be useful to have available learning materials, and
case studies of successful groups elsewhere, for consultation by
those attempting to establish a new group. A crucial practical
point, also, is the nomination of a contact person for each group
(who is well informed about all present and future activities of
the group) and a network of communication between contact
persons and a central point of information which can be identified
in all publicity and to all enquirers.

The OPAL worker in the University of Lancaster Extra-
Mural Studies office fulfilled the latter function for the Lancaster,
Morecambe and district U3A. A crucial issue which has run
throughout the existence hitherto of this U3A is the proper balance
to be maintained in an infant voluntary association between the
effort and initiatives of the members and the support and guidance
of the public educational institution which provided the original
dynamic. Members of this U3A association were very happy to
accept whatever help the University and the Manpower Services
Commission could offer. For many, the ideas of self-help and
self-direction were means rather than ends; the major goals
were increasing the accessibility to themselves, and to others
like them, of actual learning opportunities (however provided)
and of improving their access to major educational facilities
such as those of the local University. Thus, in the period under
question, there was little internal thrust in the Lancaster,
Morecambe and district U3A towards independence and self-
support. In the long run, it may prove to be a bad thing for so
many of the original U3A functions to have been carried out by
the paid, almost full-time MSC OPAL worker, based in the
University. It may be that the close (in some ways dependent)
relationship between the local U3A and the University of
Lancaster will have been irretrievably institutionalised. Yet the
nearby and contemporaneous impressive local experience of the
Caton and Brookhouse Creative Leisure Activities Association
shows that self-help and self-dependence among groups of older
persons can work remarkably well.

Of course, it can easily be seen that the Lancaster, Morecambe and district U3A entered into the political arena as soon
as it grew to a certain size and organised a press campaign.
Statutory providers of adult education are conscious of their

marginal claims on the public purse and their marginal status in
the public mind. They are badly affected by public expenditure
cuts, staff and material resource reductions and declining morale.
Some providers in the Lancaster area were understandably (and,
therefore, in that sense rightly) irritated and worried by the brash
and successful local U3A press publicity. It is interesting that
the perceptions of some of them were of a parvenue amateur
'provider' entering into competition for what was believed to be
the limited pool of adults available for participation in class-room
based adult education. Moreover, according to these perceptions,
the newcomer was using unfair means - it could advertise itself
as free because (unlike the Responsible Bodies) it had free access
to certain accommodation and (unlike all of them) it did not insist
on professional standards of paid tuition.

Evidently these perceptions were inappropriate and misin-
formed. But with hindsight it can be claimed that the reaction
of some of the statutory providers was predictable and could
have been prevented. The University of Lancaster's Extra-
Mural Studies office and the local U3A committee could have
consulted and informed the local providers in advance of the
press campaign. For U3A associations and groups, properly
understood, are not in competition with statutory providers.
Rather, they are concerned with educational concepts and
practices which do not predominate in formal provision. When
all statutory providers accept that adult learning does not
necessarily have to be institutionalised, professionalised
'provided' and contained in a 'programme', when the real
physical and material barriers between older people and access
to formal educational opportunities are removed, when the needs
of older people for learning involvement and their potential as
educators and educational resources are generally recognised,
then - but not before then - will it be legitimate to question
whether the existence of 'University of the Third Age' associations and groups is justified.

Keith Percy's conclusions could well serve for the whole
of this study, for he very properly brings us full circle.
U3A groups are, as he reminds, 'concerned with educational
concepts and practices which do not predominate in formal
provision'. Indeed, they were developed, in part, because
of that inadequacy and, indirectly, as a standing reminder
of that absence. When the golden day dawns upon which
Keith Percy's three obstacles - institutionalised programming,
barriers to access, the non-acknowledgment of 'elderly'
potential - are removed, then will the distinction between

state and self-help provision be pleasingly blurred. All U3As will begin to look like schools and colleges, and all the schools and colleges will begin to look like U3As. What Michael Young called 'the grand sharing between all the citizens of the nation' would be the glorious outcome. These U3A activists hope that the tiny steps described here are steps in that direction. We have outlined the theory and detailed the practice, for much thought as well as much activity has gone into the primitive stirrings of British U3As. But deliberately, no attempt has been made to judge to what extent their practical implementation has matched the designs and aims of the idealogues. It is for others to assess the present degree of compatibility between ideal and actuality. Suffice it to say that, as for the future, U3A activists are determined to clarify the definitions by relation to practice, and improve the application by reference to sharper analysis of the idea.

INDEX

For Product Safety Concerns and Information please contact our EU
representative GPSR@taylorandfrancis.com
Taylor & Francis Verlag GmbH, Kaufingerstraße 24, 80331 München, Germany